Learning Language Arts Through Literature

THE GOLD BOOK

American Literature

By

Greg Strayer, Ph.D.

Common Sense Press
TM

The *Learning Language Arts Through Literature* series:

The Blue Book - 1st Grade Skills
The Red Book - 2nd Grade Skills
The Yellow Book - 3rd Grade Skills
The Orange Book - 4th Grade Skills
The Purple Book - 5th Grade Skills
The Tan Book - 6th Grade Skills
The Green Book - 7th Grade Skills
The Gray Book - 8th Grade Skills
The Gold Book - American Literature - High School Skills
The Gold Book - British Literature - High School Skills

Scripture taken from the NEW AMERICAN STANDARD BIBLE®
©Copyright The Lockman Foundation
1960,1962,1963,1968,1971,1972,1973,1975,1977
Used by permission.

Copyright ©2000 by:
Common Sense Press, Inc.
8786 Highway 21
Melrose, FL 32666
www.commonsensepress.com

Printed in the United States of America.

Rev 08/11
Printed 08/11

ISBN 978-1-880892-89-3

Introduction

The Gold Book - American Literature is written in a style that provides instructions and directions for the student and teacher in an easy-to-use format. Thought provoking questions and answers guide the student and teacher into learning experiences filled with opportunities for critical thinking and analysis. We highly value the teacher's opportunity to help shape and develop her student's understanding and beliefs, so we encourage discussion on issues raised in the literature. The poems, short stories, essays, and novels examined in this manual have been selected to demonstrate literary principles. The authors of these selections are considered among the best of American authors and represent a fruitful time in literary history. Upon consideration of these authors, please note that these authors and their works are secular. While their works are not religious in nature, the topics they consider raise questions that can and should be answered out of the context of faith.

We suggest that the teacher read over the literature and the questions to determine whether or not any content or questions may be of concern. We do not necessarily recommend the other literature selections in the collections of short stories and poems and encourage the teacher to evaluate them prior to having them read by the student.

Learning Language Arts Through Literature, *The Gold Book - American Literature,* is written as a college preparation course that may be used at any high school level. We are pleased to present this excellent manual for teacher and student.

How to Use This Book

The Gold Book - American Literature is designed to be used by the student and the teacher. It is organized by units:

Unit 1 - The Short Story
Unit 2 - The Novel
Unit 3 - The Essay
Unit 4 - Poetry

Each lesson consists of a five day week, complete with assignments and questions. *Teacher Helps* are located at the end of each lesson for easy reference. Many of the questions may be answered orally or as a written assignment. We encourage the teacher to vary requirements for oral or written answers depending on what will best assist the student in learning. We also suggest adjusting reading assignments to meet the student's needs. If the student requires more time to read a short story or novel, the lessons may be adjusted accordingly.

In conclusion, we hope this language arts course will encourage the high school student's ability to read and understand literature as well as develop the ability for verbal and written expression. It is also our desire that the student be able to interpret and assess literary meaning in terms of content and philosophy, and then be able to clearly state a position in response. As the student's understanding of literature grows, it is our prayer that there will be equal growth in the ability to "give an account for the hope that is within you."

To complete the assignments in this manual, the student will need the following books and a Bible. Scripture passages in this manual are from the *New American Standard Bible* unless otherwise noted.

Great American Short Stories, edited by Wallace and Mary Stegner, published by Random House
ISBN 9780440330608

The Red Badge of Courage, by Stephen Crane, published by Random House
ISBN 9780553210118

The Old Man and the Sea, by Ernest Hemingway, published by Simon & Schuster ISBN 9780684801223

The Pearl, by John Steinbeck, published by Penguin Group ISBN 9780140177374

The Mentor Book of Major American Poets, edited by Oscar Williams and Edwin Honig, published by Penguin Books ISBN 9780451627919

Table of Contents

UNIT 1

The Short Story

The Short Story Unit

Before you begin, read the objectives listed with your student. It is helpful to understand what the student is expected to learn in each section.

In conjunction with the lessons in *The Gold Book* it is suggested that the student keep a notebook divided into four sections. The first section is for various short writing assignments that will appear in the lessons. The second section is for vocabulary words that the student will be asked to define. In The Short Story Unit these words will appear the first day of each lesson and will be reviewed on the last day. The third section is to record definitions for the literary terms that are introduced throughout the lessons. A list of these terms is provided at the beginning of each unit. When the term is presented for the first time, it will be in bold print, along with its definition. A list of these terms is found in the back of this book. The fourth section is reserved for the short stories and essays your student will be writing.

The questions asked in the lessons are designed to be interactive. Be sure to spend some time discussing the answers with your student.

In The Short Story Unit, you will read the following short stories from *Great American Short Stories*, edited by Wallace and Mary Stegner, published by Random House ISBN 9780440330608.

The Real Thing	by Henry James
The Open Boat	by Stephen Crane
Unlighted Lamps	by Sherwood Anderson
The Catbird Seat	by James Thurber
To the Mountains	by Paul Horgan
Young Goodman Brown	by Nathaniel Hawthorne
The Fall of the House of Usher	by Edgar Allan Poe
Bartleby the Scrivener	by Herman Melville
Baker's Bluejay Yarn	by Mark Twain (Samuel Clemens)
A Village Singer	by Mary Wilkins Freeman

Objectives

1) to expand the student's knowledge of what constitutes a short story
2) to examine the elements of a short story
3) to help the student identify and analyze the characters portrayed in a short story
4) to familiarize the student with famous American short story authors
5) to incorporate elements learned in producing the student's own short stories

Terms to Identify

short story
character
characterization
direct method
indirect method
narrator
conflict
internal conflict
external conflict
flat character
round character
climax
allusion
foreshadowing
irony
plot
exposition
rising action
falling action
resolution

symbol
realism
romanticism
mood
point of view
first person point of view
second person point of view
third person point of view
context clues
editorializing
third person objective
third person omniscient
third person limited omniscient
rough draft
final copy
idiom
allegory
dialect
suspense
imagery
compare

1. a. What is a **short story** and how does it differ from a novel, research paper, poem, or biography?

   b. Henry James was a nineteenth century author who was a master of diversity in writing style. In his stories he is known for presenting a complex problem and challenging the reader to solve it as the story progresses.

   c. Read "The Real Thing" by Henry James (pp. 160-190).

   d. Define the following words as used in the context of the story. The page number for the word is listed.

      1) paradoxical (p. 160)
      2) emoluments (p. 162)
      3) unanimity (p.166)

2. a. A **character** is a person who appears in the story. The author presents a character so we can determine his physical appearance and personality through a process called **characterization**. There are two methods used to describe a character in a short story:

      1) Using the **direct method**, the narrator describes a character by directly showing the readers a character's traits.

      2) Using the **indirect method**, the narrator describes a character by telling the readers about the character's appearance, what the character does and says, and how other characters react to him/her. By learning about the character indirectly, readers must draw their own conclusions about the character.

      Sometimes a combination of both methods is used.

   b. In the first few pages of the story, the author reveals some information about the Monarchs. Decide whether the author uses the direct method, the indirect method, or a combination of both. Support your answer.

   c. Find examples in Part One of the story that describe each of the Monarchs. Write a brief description for each character using the information obtained from the story.

d. Look over "The Real Thing" Part One (pp. 160-166), and write a short paragraph describing the **narrator**, the person telling the story. You will have to do this by observing him and his surroundings. For example, the narrator's servant announces the arrival of the Monarchs. You can make judgments based on how the narrator observes and treats the Monarchs. What does that show you about the narrator's social position?

e. The narrator handles the situation with the Monarchs in a very gracious manner. What do these actions reveal about his character?

. a. Reread Part Two of "The Real Thing" (pp. 167-173).

b. One of the elements of a short story is the conflict. The **conflict** is the element that makes the story interesting to the reader. Usually a conflict involves an obstacle that one or more characters must overcome. Conflicts are classified as being either an **internal conflict** (a character's struggles within himself) or **external conflict** (a character's struggles with outside forces). Traditionally, the main character is the person with a conflict.

A conflict may be classified as:
1) man vs. man
2) man vs. nature
3) man vs. himself
4) man vs. God

Identify which of the conflicts listed above are internal and which are external.

Without a conflict, the writing is a documentary, a narrative, or a description, but not a story.

c. Describe the conflict in "The Real Thing."

d. Using the information in **3b**, how would you classify this conflict?

e. As we learn more about the Monarchs, the conflicts are heightened. At what point in Part Two do you find the fullest extent of the Monarchs' situation?

f. How does this increase the narrator's conflict?

g. The **setting** of a story is the time period and place where the story takes place. In "The Real Thing" the setting is in the late 1800's in England, probably London. The author, Henry James, was living in London during this time. Research this time period as to social structure and events that could have caused the Monarchs to lose their money.

4. a. On page 171, you are introduced to a new character, Miss Churm. Write a character description of Miss Churm in the same way you did for the Monarchs.

b. Let's compare the character of Miss Churm to the Monarchs. Miss Churm is what we call a **flat character**. She is one-dimensional and never changes. The Monarchs, on the other hand, are multifaceted and possess considerable depth. Characters who are well-developed and have many sides are called **round characters**. What sort of character would you consider the narrator to be? Explain how you came to your conclusion.

c. Reread Part Three of "The Real Thing" (pp. 173-180).

d. The narrator is unable to paint the Monarchs any differently than they actually are. "She was the real thing, but always the same thing" (p.175). However, he seems able to paint Miss Churm as any character he wants. What are some reasons for this?

e. Why does the narrator refer to the Monarchs as "the real thing" in the story? What makes them real?

f. How does the conflict escalate in Part Three?

5. a. Reread Part Four of "The Real Thing" (pp. 181-190).

b. Would you classify Jack Hawley (p.183) as a flat or round character? Why?

c. In the paragraph beginning on page 186 and ending on page 187, the narrator reverses the roles of the Monarchs and their servant, Oronte, three times. What are these three reversals?

d. The **climax** of the story is the turning point of the conflict. Often the climax contains intense emotion. Using the information you have just gathered, what is the climax of the crisis that has been building?

e. Why does the narrator draw the Monarchs as having great size?

f. On page 190, reread part of the last page, beginning with the sentence, "They had accepted their failure, but they couldn't accept their fate." The narrator is summarizing the meaning of the story. What do you think he is saying?

g. Due to circumstances beyond their control, the Monarchs can no longer maintain their identity based on wealth and position. [Many people today face situations such as job loss, relocating to distant places, or economic pressures. Observing the Monarchs' loss of identity based on circumstances, what do you feel should be the basis of your identity? Write several paragraphs outlining your beliefs regarding the source of your true identity.]

h. Complete the following sentences using one of the vocabulary words: paradoxical, emoluments, unanimity.

   1) To say the forest can be saved by burning seems like a
      _____ statement.
   2) The classroom echoed with the students' cheers of
      _____ at the teacher's suggestion to postpone the test.
   3) At the end of the day _____ were distributed for the work done.

1.

a. A short story is a fictional writing in prose form that has a limited number of characters, brings forth a single emotional effect, and can usually be read in a single sitting.

d.

1) paradoxical – that which seems conflicting with common sense

2) emolument - compensation received for work done

s3) unanimity - a united opinion or agreement

2.

b. The author uses both the direct and indirect method. Answers will vary, but the following are examples of support.

direct - "She was slim, and so well-dressed."

indirect - "Sketch her off, you know," said the gentlemen, coloring.
His embarrassment lets you know he is a proud man who obviously finds the situation difficult.

c. Mrs. Monarch - Mrs. Monarch is a tall, slender, well dressed older woman of obvious good breeding. Despite their present financial distress, she has a regal way of presenting herself in her mannerisms and speech. She also is somewhat shy and always shows submissiveness and admiration toward her husband.

Major Monarch - Mr. Monarch, a retired army major, is approximately 50 years of age. He is a well dressed, tall man with a mustache. He possesses a dignified and proud bearing often associated with a person of position in society. Obviously much in love with his wife, he always speaks of her with praise and affection.

d. It shows you he is wealthy, a man of social position.

e. The narrator possesses the qualities of kindness and understanding. He understands the Monarchs' hardship and is sensitive to their feelings. Despite their lack of finances, he treats them with respect.

3.

b.

1) man vs. man - external

2) man vs. nature - external

3) man vs. himself - internal

4) man vs. God - external / internal

c. The conflict is twofold:

1) the conflict the Monarchs have in dealing with their loss of social position and need for employment

2) the conflict the narrator has of employing them, not because he needs them as models, but because he feels obligated to help them

d. Both conflicts can be classified as man vs. himself.

e. The paragraph on pp. 170-171 in which Major Monarch confesses he has "tried everything," and Mrs. Monarch bursts into tears.

f. He realizes they are desperate for some sort of employment and feels obligated to help them.

g. The time period of this story is England during the Industrial Revolution. Work that was once done by hand in the home or on small farms was now done in factories. Society in England changed drastically during this period with many peasant farmers coming to the large cities to find work in factories. Factories were owned by the wealthy who used the cheap labor to increase their profits. Social status at this time became based more on a person's financial status than on the basis of his upbringing and position.

The Monarchs could have lost their money by investing in a factory that went bankrupt or a shipping venture.

4.

a. Miss Churm is quite a contrast to Mrs. Monarch. Small and freckled, Miss Churm lacks dignity and respectability. She is uneducated and unrefined in her behavior. The author points out her inability to spell and her love for beer. However, she possesses the ability to act and become any character the narrator wishes her to become for his purpose of artwork.

b. The narrator would be considered a round character as his character has many aspects and develops along with the story. At first he is rather optimistic about his ability to use the Monarchs as models but later realizes their limited abilities. He knows he must face the fact that although he is fond of and respects the Monarchs, he cannot use them as models or it will mean his ruin as an illustrator.

d. The Monarchs are unable to assume poses that represent other characters (bottom p. 175), whereas Miss Churm is like an actress, and can become a different character upon request (bottom p. 176). This is due largely to their differences in social class. The Monarchs seem unable to step outside the character suitable to their social class, whereas Miss Churm has nothing to lose.

4.

e. As the Major ingenuously refers to himself and his wife on page 170, they are, in fact, the real thing. He is the perfect gentleman (p. 164), and she, the perfect lady. Despite their financial hardship, the narrator can hardly see them as anything else. Other painters' models, like the cockney Miss Churm, can become a lady for a picture, but the Monarchs find it impossible to be anything but what they are in real life.

f. The Monarchs are less useful to the narrator than he had thought. Furthermore, his sense of obligation to help them increases. (Read the last eight lines on page 178.)

5.

b. Jack Hawley is a flat character with only one purpose in the story: to confirm the narrator's suspicion that the Monarchs are not acceptable as models.

c.

1) He uses Oronte for Rutland Ramsay instead of Major Monarch.
2) He visualizes the Major as a footman instead of Oronte.
3) He requires Mrs. Monarch to serve tea to Oronte, the servant, while he is sitting.

d. The climax is when the Major asks if they can be the narrator's servants.

e. The narrator sees the Monarchs as "larger than life" because of their social class and fabulous life background.

f. The Monarchs had accepted the fact that they were failures as models. It is more difficult for them to accept that they can no longer keep their social position. To keep from starving, they must lower their position to serve others.

g. Answers will vary.

h.
1) paradoxical
2) unanimity
3) emoluments

1. a. Stephen Crane (1871-1900) wrote "The Open Boat" in 1898. (More information about Stephen Crane is found in Lesson 27.) Enjoy reading "The Open Boat" (pp. 257-286).

   b. Define the following words as used in the context of the story. The page number for the word is listed.

      1) gunwale (p. 257)
      2) dinghy (p. 259)
      3) aberrations (p. 265)

2. a. An important element of fiction that is often overlooked is the setting of a story. Sometimes the reader becomes so involved in the characters that the role the setting plays in the story is taken for granted or ignored.

      Look over Part One of "The Open Boat" (pp. 257-260), and notice how the setting is vital to the progress of the drama.

   b. What is the conflict in this story?

   c. How would you classify this conflict? (See Lesson 1, **3b**).

   d. Identify four pieces of information that the author uses to let the reader know that the men are in extreme danger.

   e. Why is the setting such an important element of this story?

   f. At the beginning of "The Open Boat," the following statement appears:

      "A tale intended to be after the fact. Being the experience of four men from the sunk steamer "Commodore."

      What does this tell you about this story?

   g. Do you think it is based on a real-life event?

   h. Above this statement, dates appear which tell when the author lived. Does knowing when Stephen Crane lived help you to place the time period of this story?

i. Do some research about the author, Stephen Crane. Determine how a real-life experience of Crane's helped him obtain information for writing "The Open Boat."

j. Why did he include the correspondent as one of his characters?

3. a. Reread Part Two of "The Open Boat" (pp. 260-263).

b. In the first paragraph of Part Two, what two sides of nature are shown? Explain.

c. What two sides are there to the action of the wind?

d. Find two sentences in Part Two page 261, one directly following the other, that clearly show this contrast.

e. At the bottom of page 261, the men see the gulls as "grewsome (gruesome) and ominous." Is this a true perception?

What caused them to come to this conclusion?

f. What conclusions can you make about Crane's representation of nature in this story?

g. Write a few paragraphs contrasting and comparing the two aspects of nature as discussed in **3b**. Use a quote from the story to support each view.

4. a. Reread Part Three of "The Open Boat" (pp. 263-266).

b. In this part of the story the conflict is both heightened and lessened. Following the sequence of events, write a list of ways in which the conflict is heightened or lessened.

c. What was the significance of the men smoking a cigar together?

d. Look at a map of Florida. Find the area marked Mosquito Inlet. Is it on the Atlantic or Gulf of Mexico coast of Florida?

e. How would their location affect the type of surf they would have to deal with?

f. Why was it impossible for them to row ashore without the dinghy swamping?

5. a. A good description of the relationship between the four characters is given in the first paragraph of Part Three. Using the information given there and in the first two parts of the story, write a brief description of each character. Include each character's strengths and weaknesses as a member of the team.

b. Often a team of good athletes fails because they refuse to work together. What evidence supports that the four characters in the boat have learned to work well as a team?

c. Reread Part Four of "The Open Boat" (pp. 266-273).

d. At the top of page 268, the correspondent makes reference to "Fate." What do you think the author means by Fate?

e. List three examples from Part Four as evidence of the way Fate is shaping their outcome.

f. Use the vocabulary words to complete the following sentences: gunwale, dinghy, aberrations.

   1) The teacher's _____ made it difficult to comprehend what he was trying to say.
   2) The boy clutched the _____ in order to keep from being thrown overboard.
   3) The _____ was too small to safely hold the four men.

1.

b.

    1) gunwale - the upper edge of the side of a boat

    2) dinghy - a small boat usually carried on a large ship for emergency purposes

    3) aberrations - deviations from what is normal or typical

2.

b. The conflict in this story is the men in a boat fighting for survival against the forces of nature.

c. This conflict would be classified as man vs. nature.

d. Answers may vary, but the following are possible answers:

    1) The men can't see shore.

    2) The waves are "barbarously huge."

    3) The boat is very small, only ten feet.

    4) One man is injured and can't help.

    5) They are taking in water and have to keep bailing it out.

    6) The oars are small and seem fragile.

e. The setting in this story sets the stage for all the other events to take place; it is the key element. If the setting were to change, the story would change.

f. The statement tells you the story was written after the incident occurred.

g. It seems to inform you that the story was based on a real-life experience.

h. The dates showing when the author lived helps you to place the setting of the story during that time period.

i. The following information may be helpful:
Crane was headed for Cuba in a ship that left Jacksonville, Florida, in January, 1896. When the ship wrecked, Crane and three other men were adrift in a dinghy for a period of 30 hours. His experience was used as the basis for "The Open Boat."

j. The correspondent is included as one of the characters because he represents Crane.

3.

b. First the dangerous side of nature is shown by how the boat is being tossed about by the winds and high surf. Secondly, the beauty of nature is also shown by the author's description of "... this play of the free sea, wild with lights of emerald and white and amber..."

c. On one side, the wind is helping to push them towards the shore. On the other side, it is so strong they are in danger of the boat filling up with water and sinking from the high surf. Also the surf becomes rougher as they row nearer to shore, and they will be in danger of the boat capsizing.

4.

b.

Lessened:
 1) The men form a cooperative team against the common foes.
 2) They make a successful sail.
 3) They get closer to shore.
 4) They spot the house of refuge.
 5) They are only an hour away from shore.

Heightened:
 1) The life saving station might be abandoned.
 2) The wind dies down, and they can't sail any longer.
 3) The men haven't slept or eaten in over two days.

c. Often smoking together at the end of a difficult task is symbolic of the task being accomplished and victory being at hand.

d. It is located on the Atlantic coast of Florida.

e. The surf would be much higher and rougher on the Atlantic side than on the Gulf of Mexico side.

f. Since the surf becomes rougher as you near the shore, it was almost impossible for them to row ashore in such a small boat without capsizing.

l. ... so the oiler quoth: "Yes! If this wind holds!"

The cook was bailing: "Yes! If we don't catch hell in the surf."

. No, the gulls are a harmless nuisance.

They perceive them as grewsome (gruesome) and ominous because of their resentment towards the sea and nature in general. They have the feeling, irrational though it might be, that nature is fighting against them, wanting to destroy them.

. The conclusion is that nature is not good, bad, kind, or hostile. Natural forces exist without any special direction or force behind them.

g. Quote to support the bad aspects of nature:
"... Occasionally a great spread of water, like white flames, swarmed into her..." (p. 263).

Quote to support the good aspects of nature:
"... It was probably splendid. It was probably glorious, this play of the free sea, wild with lights of emerald and white and amber..." (p. 260).

5.

a. captain - Even though he is hurt and physically unable to assist with keeping the small dinghy afloat, the captain continually watches out for the safety of the crew. He is ever vigilant, calm, and wise in every situation the crew must deal with. He is the person who continually rallies and encourages the others.

oiler - The greatest assets the oiler brings to the situation are his strong back and experience. His character is one of a proud, determined spirit who does not give up. However, he tends to rely too much on himself and his own strength and does not lean on the others for support.

cook - The cook is a very willing worker who does whatever is asked of him without complaint. Being overweight and out of shape makes it hard for him to carry the same share of the workload as the oiler and correspondent, but he does what he can by keeping the boat bailed.

correspondent - Although having a somewhat cynical nature, the correspondent is still a very cooperative member of the crew, always doing what is asked of him. He is physically strong and is able to do a good share of the rowing. Being pessimistic, however, he tends to view the ocean as an enemy that is out to get the small crew.

b. They all share the work and no one wastes energy arguing or complaining about what is fair. They know they must cooperate if they are to have any chance of making it safely ashore.

d. The author sees Fate as a force beyond our control which shapes our lives by the circumstances we must deal with, some good and some bad. However, he does give Fate a personality, as if "she" were making a decision as to whether or not to drown him.

e. Possible answers:
1) There is no life saving station.
2) The surf is too rough for them to get close enough to shore.
3) The oiler is able to turn them back to sea without capsizing the boat.
4) The only people who see them are a group of tourists who do nothing to help them.

f.
1) aberrations
2) gunwale
3) dinghy

1. a. Reread Part Five of "The Open Boat" (pp. 273-276).

   b. How does the correspondent view the sleeping men in the bottom of the boat?

   c. What is the correspondent's impression of the shark that circled them? What is his feeling toward the sea and nature in general? Support your answer with examples from the story.

   d. Do you think these are rational feelings? How do they compare with the men's response to the circling gulls earlier in the story?

   e. Define the following words as used in the context of the story. The page number for the word is listed.

      1) bequeathed (p. 279)
      2) beneficent (p. 280)
      3) coerce (p. 281)

2. a. Reread Part Six of "The Open Boat" (pp. 276-280).

   b. From the middle of page 277 to the middle of page 278, the correspondent reminisces about a verse he knew from childhood. When a familiar piece of literature, Bible story, person, or historical event is referenced in literature it is called an allusion. By using an **allusion**, the author can have the reader recall an entire story or event with just a few words or lines. How does the allusion add to the story?

      Would it have been more difficult for the author to convey his thoughts to the reader without referencing the verse?

   c. Why does the correspondent's attitude toward the dying legionnaire change?

d. Experiencing a hard situation often helps you to sympathize with someone else who is going through a similar situation. Have you ever had a difficult time that taught you to be more sympathetic to someone else's problems? Tell your teacher about one example in your life.

e. **Foreshadowing** is a method used by the author to give hints or suggestions to the reader of coming events. How does the poem about the legionnaire foreshadow how the story might end?

3. a. Reread Part Seven of "The Open Boat" (pp. 280-286).

b. **Irony** is a literary device that reveals a reality other than what seems to be true. A turn of events may give unexpected results. What is the irony of this story?

c. Why is the oiler the least likely to die?

d. Why do you think the oiler is the only named character in the story?

e. All the other men took hold of life saving objects except the oiler. Was the oiler's act foolish or heroic? Explain how you came to your conclusion.

f. The author described his view of the world as being controlled by fate. How is this view different to the view of God governing events and circumstances?

g. Write a few paragraphs comparing these two views. Use Scripture to support your views.

. a. Every story has a plot. The **plot** is the sequence of events and actions that take place in the story. Every good plot contains five main elements:

1) Exposition - The **exposition** introduces the characters, explains the background of the story, the setting, and the present situation.
2) Rising Action - The **rising action** consists of a series of problems and struggles which build toward a climax.
3) Climax - The **climax** is the turning point, or action peak, of the story. Usually this is the point when the action and anticipation are the fullest.
4) Falling Action - The **falling action** is when the action of the turning point or high point is worked out and a solution is at hand.
5) Resolution - The **resolution** is the part of the story in which the solution comes to a conclusion, and the problem is solved. This usually provides the story with its ending.

b. The **plot line** is a graphic representation of the elements of a plot. This may help you to better understand how the parts of the plot fit together.

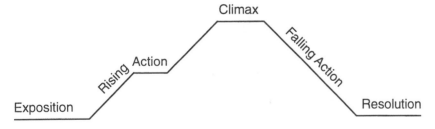

c. Look over "The Open Boat." Identify the parts of the story and write a brief summary statement of each.

5. a. The idea or statement which a story is about is called the **theme.** As the story unfolds, we analyze the characters and their conflicts and unravel the themes of the story. Usually a story has a main theme that can be identified.

   b. What is the main theme in "The Open Boat"? Support your conclusion with examples from the story.

   c. What does the statement, "Yes, but I love myself," that appears on p. 277 reveal to the reader about how the author feels about the conflict between man and nature?

   d. Use the correct vocabulary word to complete the following sentences: bequeathed, beneficent, coerce.

      1) The official will _____him into giving a true statement.
      2) He was a _____ brother who always looked ou for the safety of his younger brothers and sisters.
      3) In his will he _____ all his belongings to his young nephew.

1.

b. The way they had snuggled together sleeping on the bottom of the boat made the correspondent think of them as "babes of the sea."

c. The correspondent views the shark as having almost magical characteristics. He admires the shark's beauty while at the same time hating everything in nature it represents to him. For example, he describes the shark's appearance as "a gleaming trail of phosphorescence, like blue flame," and also mentions "the speed and power of the thing was greatly to be admired." However, his feelings of anger toward the sea and nature are not changed by this appearance. Even though the correspondent is not afraid of the shark, he feels alienated from it and curses it, "He simply looked at the sea dully and swore in an undertone."

d. His feelings are not based on rational reasoning. In the same way the men resented the presence of the gulls earlier in the story, the men resent the appearance of the shark. The men see the ocean and nature as fighting against them, and they resent any living thing that seems to be in harmony with nature.

e.
1) bequeathed - to give to another person; to pass something on to another
2) beneficent - kind; doing good
3) coerce - to force or compel to do something

2.

b. It causes the reader to make a correlation between the suffering of the legionnaire and the suffering of the men on the boat. Each was dying in a place far from home with only his companions for comfort.

Without use of the verse it would be hard for the author to convey this idea to the reader.

c. When he read the words of the verse before, he was unable to relate to the suffering of the legionnaire. Now that he is suffering in a similar way, he is able to better understand the legionnaire's suffering as is evidenced by the statement, "He was sorry for the soldier of the Legion who lay dying in Algiers."

d. Allow for discussion.

e. The verse about the legionnaire suggests that one or all of the men in the boat may die.

3.

b. The irony of this story is that the oiler, who is the person least likely to die in the attempt to swim to shore, is the person who dies in his attempt.

c. The oiler is a strong man who has done more than his share of the rowing and is also a strong swimmer. He is described as "The wily surfman" so he is knowledgeable about the ways of the ocean and how to handle himself in it. This makes him the least likely character to die. It was more probable that the overweight cook, the injured captain, or the correspondent, who has little sea experience, would die.

d. The oiler, whose name was Billie, was the only named character. The author may have done this for the purpose of making the character more real to the reader, and therefore, adding to the irony of him being the only character who does not make it successfully to shore.

e. There are two viewpoints for this question, with strong evidence on both sides. The oiler has been unselfish and worked hard to assure everyone the best chance of making it to shore, yet at the last moment he strikes out on his own, leaving the others behind.

This seems to contradict the steadfast, faithful character that had been portrayed thus far. However, perhaps the oiler was thinking of the others and decided he would not be a burden by adding weight to the capsized boat. It already had a tremendous amount to hold afloat, and he felt that he could make it ashore without assistance.

f. The author sees fate as being in control of his destiny. He believes the events and circumstances he must deal with as being random with no one truly in control of what happens in his life. This is the opposite of the Christian viewpoint that God is in control of every event and circumstance and nothing happens by chance.

.

. Answers will vary but should include the following basic information.

1) **Exposition** - In the exposition part of this story the author immediately lets you know that the small crew has been shipwrecked, and the setting for the story is a small dinghy adrift in the ocean. Four characters, the captain, the cook, the oiler, and the correspondent, are introduced to the reader.

2) **Rising Action** - The rising action of the story tells how the characters battle the waves, come within sight of shore, and conclude there is no rescue crew to help them.

3) **Climax** - The climax of the story comes when the crew is forced to try to make it to shore and the boat capsizes, spilling all the men into the ocean.

4) **Falling Action** - The falling action of the story includes how each of the characters chooses a way to make it to shore and the swimmer's attempts to help them.

5) **Resolution** - The resolution of the story includes each man making it to shore, even the oiler who died in his attempt, and onlookers assisting them.

5.

b. The main theme of this story is that man and nature are in conflict. However, as beautiful as nature might be, it is still dangerous and mysterious, and man is puny in comparison to its power.

Sample supporting statements (others may be used):
"... it occurs to a man that nature does not regard him as important, and that she feels she would not maim the universe by disposing of him ..."

"She seemed just a wee thing wallowing, miraculously top-up, at the mercy of the five oceans."

c. However unimportant man might be to nature's forces and plans, man still feels himself to be important. He feels that his life should not be treated as insignificant as is evidenced by the statement, "Yes, but I love myself."

d.
   1) coerce
   2) beneficent
   3) bequeathed

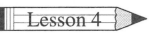

1. a. Sherwood Anderson is one of America's best and most popular storytellers. Most of his stories revolve around his home town of Camden, Ohio. Using this small town as a base, Anderson was able to translate the episodes of the town's citizens into a wide range of story and theme.

   b. Read "Unlighted Lamps" by Sherwood Anderson (pp. 287-308).

   c. Define the following words from the story.

      1) gesticulated (p. 289)
      2) antagonism (p. 292)
      3) inanimate (p. 293)

2. a. Look over Part One of "Unlighted Lamps" (begins on p. 287 and ends with the break on p. 296).

   b. What is the conflict in this story? How would you classify this conflict?

   c. Is the setting of the story important to the outcome?

   d. Describe the character, Duke Yetter, and explain how he heightens the conflict.

   e. Why does Mary enjoy walking through the rough neighborhood in the upper part of town? Give a sentence from the story that supports your answer.

   f. How do the rumors concerning Mary's mother add to her desire to escape from town? Give a sentence from the story that supports your answer.

   g. Often an author uses people or things as **symbols** for ideas he wishes to relate to the reader. The fight that breaks out between the two boys (p. 291) symbolizes the conflict between Mary and the townspeople. Which boy is the symbol for the townspeople and which is the symbol for Mary? Explain your answer. (More information on symbols is found in Lesson 28, **2g**.)

   What does this tell you about the way Mary feels?

h. Why does Mary react so angrily to Duke Yetter's intrusion?

i. In viewing this area of town through Mary's eyes, does she feel there is a definite line that divides classes of people? Support your answer with examples from the text.

j. Do you feel that a class system still exists today? Is it different in any way? Write a few paragraphs explaining your viewpoint.

. a. Reread Part Two of "Unlighted Lamps" (begins on p. 296 and ends with the break on p. 299).

b. It is evident that Mary has led a very isolated life. Based on what you have read, is this isolation entirely due to the way she is treated by the townspeople or is it somewhat due to her response to others? Support your answer with examples from the story.

c. What does the laborer's story reveal to us about the relationship between Mary and her father?

d. How is Mary affected by the laborer's story?

. a. Reread Part Three of "Unlighted Lamps" (begins on p. 299 and ends with the break on p. 304).

b. What does the scene regarding Dr. Cochran's sending away his wife reveal about the relationship between him and Mary?

c. What does the scene about the announcement of his wife's pregnancy further reveal about Dr. Cochran's feelings? Why is he unable to show affection? Support your answer with sentences from the story.

d. Two types of literature are realism and romanticism. **Realism** describes a story in which the author gives a realistic view of life. It usually involves everyday people and does not necessarily have a "happy ending." **Romanticism** is based more on an imaginary view of life, with heroes and happy endings. Would you classify "Unlighted Lamps" as realism or romanticism? Why?

e. "Unlighted Lamps" is part of a collection of short stories entitled *Winesburg, Ohio* by Sherwood Anderson. The author felt the stories belonged together and should be read collectively rather than separately.

Optional: Locate the book, *Winesburg, Ohio*, at your library and read other selections. Do you agree with the author that they should be read as a complete work rather than as separate short stories?

5. a. Reread Part Four of "Unlighted Lamps" (begins on p. 304 and ends on p. 308).

b. This story ends with the last chance for communication being lost. What fundamental tendency of human nature kept the doctor and his daughter from communicating with each other? Do you see this tendency in yourself and others?

c. The author of "Unlighted Lamps," Sherwood Anderson, had a major influence on early twentieth century literature. Unlike other authors, he wrote stories that focused on mood and an examination of the emotions and thoughts of the characters rather than an emphasis on the plot.

d. The **mood** of a story is based on how a piece of literature makes the reader feel. What is the mood created in "Unlighted Lamps"? What elements of the story cause this mood to be created?

e. The doctor did not have a good relationship with his daughter; in fact, they were very distant in their relationship with each other. Describe ways you feel the doctor could have made his relationship with his daughter better.

f. On p. 298 of "Unlighted Lamps," Mary has a realization about her father's life. The author refers to it as "... like a stream running always in shadows and never coming out into the sunlight." Write a paragraph explaining this line and what the author was saying about the doctor's life.

g. Using a thesaurus, write a synonym for each of the following vocabulary words:

   1) gesticulated
   2) antagonism
   3) inanimate

1.

c.

1) gesticulated - used hand or body movements to express ideas

2) antagonism - hostile feelings

3) inanimate - not alive

2.

b. The conflict is between the father and daughter and deals with the father's inability to show affection towards his daughter. This would be classified as man vs. man.

c. The setting of this story is not particularly important to the outcome. The relationship between the father and daughter could be taking place almost anywhere, which gives the story a universal appeal.

d. Duke Yetter appears to be brash and independent. His checkered suit indicates that he has the money to dress well but chooses to dress in clothes that are flashy and attract attention rather than admiration. Yetter's acceptance by the livery stable group shows that he might be out of place in more sophisticated circles.

His brash attitude and obvious interest in Mary adds to the reader's concern for her. Because of her feelings of insecurity, she might be vulnerable to his advances, and her father, being wrapped up in a world of his own, would be unable to protect her.

e. Mary enjoys walking through the rough neighborhood because it gives her a sense of adventure, as well as a sense of escape from the old town where she grew up.

Supporting statement: "To be in the street made her feel that she had gone out of her town and on a voyage into a strange land" (p. 292).

f. The townspeople's attitude toward Mary is shaped by the scandal involving her mother's sudden departure.

Supporting statement: "She'll turn out bad. Like mother, like daughter" (p. 294).

g. The red-haired boy, who is physically described so as to represent strength and power, symbolizes the townspeople. The pale, weaker boy who does not have a mother to come to his aid to defend him symbolizes Mary.

This tells you that Mary feels helpless in her dealing with the townspeople. She feels that no one will come to her defense; she has been abandoned.

2.

h. Duke Yetter reminds her of the young man who allegedly ran away with her mother. Therefore, the anger she has inside her towards the man who took her mother away is directed at Duke (See pp. 295-296).

i. By viewing the town through Mary's eyes, you can see a definite class difference between the factory district and those who live in the eastern part of town where she lives. She sees one group as poor and made up mostly of immigrants, while in her part of town lives "the merchants, clerks, lawyers and the more well-to-do American workmen of Huntersburg" (p. 292). Although she does not have a snobbish, I'm-better-than-you attitude toward those who live in the factory district, she definitely sees them as different from herself by the statement, "To be in the street made her feel that she had gone out of her town and on a voyage into a strange land" (p. 292).

j. Answers will vary.

3.

b. Mary's isolation is not due entirely to the way she is treated by the townspeople. Because of her childhood experiences and lack of affection from her father, she finds it hard to return affection. She may not even recognize friendship when it is offered. Even though she had walked through the factory district often and people often greeted her, she did not return any of their greetings but kept to herself. Also, when Duke Yetter wanted to get to know her better, she only lashed out at him in anger.
Supporting statement:
"She had kept so much to herself that she was in fact but little known" (p. 292).

c. It shows the reader how little Mary knows about her father and how distant their relationship is. She seems unaware of this side of his personality that shows kindness and generosity towards those in need (pp. 297-298).

d. She feels a renewed love for her father and a desire to be close to him (p. 298).

4.

b. He loved his wife, but he was unable to express his feelings to her. Even when he sent his wife away, the author tells us he "…had put money into her hands and in silence and without even a farewell kiss had turned and walked away" (p. 300). In the same way, even though he loves Mary, he is unable to show her any affection. When he told her about his heart disease, the author tells us "He had wanted to put his arm about his daughter's shoulder as he talked to her, but never having shown any feeling in his relations with her could not sufficiently release some tight thing in himself" (p. 289).

4.

c. When his wife announced her pregnancy, he was unresponsive, even though the announcement caused him to be "stirred as never before"(p. 302). As he thinks back on the scene he realizes he has withheld his feelings because he is afraid of expressing himself; he is afraid of looking foolish, of being hurt.

Supporting statement: "I've always been silent because I've been afraid of expressing myself — like a blundering fool. I've been a proud man and a coward" (p. 302).

d. "Unlighted Lamps" would be classified as realism because it involves a realistic view of the lives of everyday people and their struggles.

e. Answers will vary.

5.

b. The fundamental tendency to withhold our feelings out of fear that such vulnerability will result in rejection kept the doctor and his daughter from communicating with each other.

d. The mood created in "Unlighted Lamps" is a mood of depression and frustration mixed with sadness. The depression and frustration is caused by the characters' inability to communicate with one another and show affection towards one another. The sadness comes from the fact that the lack of communication and affection has ruined lives and now the chance to restore relationships is gone forever.

e. The doctor's relationship with his daughter would improve if he could just let his guard down and show affection and concern. He could do this by hugging her, talking with her, sharing his feelings, being honest with her about the relationship with his wife and what happened, and letting her know he cares about what happens to her.

f. "... like a stream running always in the shadows and never coming out into the sunlight ..." is a simile comparing the doctor living his whole life hiding from any kind of close relationship to someone hiding in the shadows. He is not without love or compassion. He is not willing to expose himself to "the sunlight," a relationship which is real and honest, because he is afraid of being hurt or rejected if he lets his true feelings be exposed.

g.

1) gesticulated - motioned
2) antagonism - hostility
3) inanimate - lifeless

a. One element of a short story which is difficult to analyze is called point of view. **Point of view** is the position the author takes in order to tell the story. This position describes a relationship between the author and his characters and between the author and the reader. Some writers want you to know what their characters think and why they think a certain way. Other writers merely want you to know what their characters do and say, then let you decide the motivation for their actions. Thus, point of view has several angles.

b. There are three points of view from which a story can be written:
   1) The **first person point of view** is limited to one character and the pronoun *I* is used.
   2) The **second person point of view** is rarely used. The author addresses the reader throughout the story and the pronoun *you* is used.
   3) The **third person point of view** is told from an all-knowing outside source. The pronouns *he* and *she* are used.

c. Once the author has decided which viewpoint will be used in the story, he must decide how much he will reveal about his characters. In the first person viewpoint the author limits himself to what the character (called the narrator) senses, how he reacts, and what he reports. Therefore, we get the story from a one-sided, limited point of view. The narrator might analyze himself or someone else, but the author must stay within the limitations of the narrator's eyes, ears, knowledge, etc.

d. Look over the stories you have read so far. Which of these stories is written from the first person point of view? How can you tell?

e. Often a student can guess at the meaning of an unfamiliar word by using context clues. **Context clues** are the other words that appear in the sentence or sentences surrounding the difficult word that help us understand its meaning. Read the following sentence; try to figure out the meaning of the word in italics using context clues.

The young *philanthropist* started a recreation center for the inner city children.

Even though you may be unsure what the word, *philanthropist*, means, you can tell by examining the context clues in the sentence that it is someone who does kind deeds for others. Look up the word in the dictionary and see how the definition compares with this conclusion.

  f. Carefully read the following three sentences which contain one word in italics. Using context clues, decide which of the following words would be a synonym for the italicized word in the sentence: impulsive, inferior, insulting.

    1) Behind Sue's back, Laura was secretly *derisive*, making unkind remarks with other friends.
    2) The teacher considered the article the student had written *execrable* compared to the fine writing he had done in the past.
    3) In a sudden, *spontaneous* moment she reached over and gave the old woman a hug.

2. a. Unlike the narrow viewpoint offered by first person, third person point of view allows the reader to have a wider range in viewing the story. The third person point of view has three different perspectives:

    1) **Third person omniscient** allows the author to have a God-like position over the story. He not only tells us what the characters do and say, but he tells us what they think and why they act a certain way. The author may choose to reveal something about a character that even the character himself doesn't know. It also allows the author to interject information that he wants you to know, but doesn't want his characters to know. He has the freedom to go in and out of the minds and motivations of his characters, to report any circumstantial information that he deems necessary without regard to time and space. Sometimes the author will add his own interpretation of the events of his story. This technique is called **editorializing.**

2) **Third person objective** allows the author to merely report the characters and events like a journalist. The author does not analyze or provide information other than the facts.

3) **Third person limited omniscient** is any view which would fall in-between the omniscient and objective points of view.

b. Review the stories you have read so far. Which of these stories is written from a third person point of view? Of the stories written from this viewpoint, decide whether they are omniscient, objective, or limited omniscient.

c. Write a paragraph about each of the three stories, "The Real Thing," "The Open Boat," and "Unlighted Lamps." In each paragraph name the point of view that was used and give reasons for your decisions. If the viewpoint is third person, indicate whether it is omniscient, limited omniscient, or objective.

3. a. In studying the three short stories you have read you know the following elements are needed for a short story: plot, conflict, characterization, point of view, setting, mood, theme.

b. It is now time for you to become the author. You will write a short story that contains the elements listed in **3a.** The first story you write will be a story that shows realism much in the same manner as the stories you have read. Follow these guidelines in preparing to write your story:

1) Decide on the subject matter you would like to write about.
2) Choose a theme and type of conflict to portray in your story.
3) Determine the setting and mood.
4) Use a plot line to map out the plot of your story.
5) Choose the characters for your story and decide what type of personality, strengths, and weaknesses each will have.
6) Decide what point of view you will use to tell the story.

c. The subject matter for your story can come from personal experience or from experiences and subjects you have been exposed to through books, movies, etc. Your story should say something about human nature; it should be a story in which others can relate to the characters and emotions you portray.

d. Make notes in preparation for writing your story following the guidelines given.

4. a. Discuss the topic for your story and basic plot with your teacher. Once you have finalized your topic, do any research necessary to be well informed about the topic you have chosen. For example, if you decide the setting of your story is a World War II battle, you need to research that time period and place.

b. Begin writing your story. Be sure to include dialogue and show characterization through both the direct and indirect method.

5. a. Continue writing your story. When you have completed your **rough draft**, have your teacher review it and make suggestions. After you have made any changes, write a **final copy.**

b. It is not necessary that your story be finished today. Continue working on it until you feel it is complete.

"The Real Thing" is written in the first person point of view. The pronoun *I* is used throughout the story.

philanthropist - one who desires to help mankind through service, gifts, etc.

1) insulting
2) inferior
3) impulsive

"The Open Boat" - third person limited omniscient
"Unlighted Lamps" - third person omniscient

"The Real Thing" is written from first person point of view. We aren't given any information about the Monarchs' life except what the artist is able to observe. Since he sees them only when they come to the studio, this is the only view we see.

"The Open Boat" is written from the third person limited omniscient point of view. Although it first appears omniscient, Crane generalizes his interpretations of the thoughts of the men in the boat except for the correspondent. With the correspondent, he goes completely into the very thoughts and motives of the individual. This is particularly evident in Parts 5 and 6 of the story where the correspondent is left alone with his thoughts.

This is a common limited omniscient pattern, to go into the mind of one of the characters, but not all.

"Unlighted Lamps" is told from the third person omniscient point of view. The author allows himself to reveal anything he wants about the characters' actions, motives, and inner thoughts. He also tells us why they act and think as they do and reveals information about the characters that even they don't know about themselves.

1. a. Read "The Catbird Seat" by James Thurber (pp. 367-378).

   b. "The Catbird Seat" is a light-hearted short story which demonstrates the fundamentals of storytelling. James Thurber is known as one of America's best-known humorists. His stories describe society's problems in a humorous way. He is quoted as saying, "Laughter could bring many things out into the open, including, I should like to put in here, the true shape and purpose of our Bill of Rights." What do you think he means by this statement?

   c. Looking over Part One of "The Catbird Seat" (begins on p. 367 and ends with the break on p. 372), briefly describe the conflict between the characters of Mr. Martin and Mrs. Barrows.

   How would you classify this conflict?

   d. In her conversation with people, Mrs. Barrows uses idioms that she probably picked up from listening to Red Barber, th Dodgers' radio announcer (who, by the way, was a real person). An **idiom** is a phrase or expression that is recognized to have a different meaning from what it literally says. One such idiom used by Mrs. Barrows is "tearing up the pea patch" which actually means "going on a rampage." List other idioms used in the story. What do you think they mean?

2. a. Using the information gathered in Part One, write a brief description of Mr. Martin and Mrs. Barrows.

   b. Does the author use the direct or indirect method of characterization or both? Give examples to support your answer.

   c. What do you discover about Mr. Martin that is so out of character for him that you find it hard to believe?

   d. Has Mrs. Barrows actually done anything to Mr. Martin which would explain such feelings of hate? Why does he feel threatened by her?

e. What is the point of view of this story? Why do we only see a one-sided view of the character of Mrs. Barrows?

f. Write a description of Mr. Martin from Mrs. Barrows' point of view. What would be her opinion of him?

. a. Reread Part Two of "The Catbird Seat" (begins on p. 372 and ends with a break on p. 375).

b. Often an author will use a sequence of events in a story to increase a reader's feeling of uncertainty regarding the outcome of the story. This technique is called **suspense** and is often used to help keep the reader interested in the story.

c. List the sequence of events in Part Two of "The Catbird Seat" that helps to build the suspense.

What part of the plot would these events be in the story?

d. What causes Mr. Martin's plans to suddenly change in this part of the story?

. a. Reread Part Three of "The Catbird Seat" (begins p. 375 and ends on p. 378).

b. At what point does the conflict reach a climax?

c. Were you surprised by the way the story ended?

d. Do you think the resolution of the story contained an element of irony? Explain.

e. How is the setting of the story important to the outcome?

f. Are the characters in this story round, flat, or both? Give reasons for your answer.

5. a. Write a paragraph explaining why "The Catbird Seat" is a good title for this story.

   b. This short story originally appeared in a magazine called *Th* *New Yorker*. Research and learn more about James Thurber life.

   c. James Thurber was also a cartoonist and illustrator. Draw t characters of Mr. Martin and Mrs. Barrows as he portrayed them in the story.

   d. Match each of the following popular idioms with its correct meaning.

Idiom	Meaning
_____ 1) a dime a dozen	A. working too hard; trying to do too much
_____ 2) keep your shirt on	B. stay calm
_____ 3) on the double	C. hurry up
_____ 4) through thick and thin	D. very inexpensive; easily available
_____ 5) burning the candle at both ends	E. be there through good and bad time

1.

b. Sometimes looking at issues in a humorous way can help you to see the real truth of the matter. Political cartoons are good examples of this.

c. Mrs. Barrows is threatening Mr. Martin's orderly world that means everything to him.

The conflict would be classified as man vs. man.

d. The following are some idioms found in the story:
"Lifting the oxcart out of the ditch" - means trying to handle too much
"Scraping around the bottom of the pickle barrel" - means looking for something to do
"Sitting in the catbird seat" - means sitting pretty, like a batter with three balls and no strikes

2.

a. Mr. Martin - a small, serious, middle-aged man who wears glasses. He is quiet, efficient, and completely dedicated to his job. He lives a very orderly and conservative life and never indulges in smoking and drinking.

Mrs. Barrows - a loud, flamboyant woman with an overbearing personality. She is arrogant and insensitive in her dealings with others.

b. The author uses the direct method of characterization.

The following are samples of support:
Although Mrs. Barrows annoys him, he never answers her except in a polite, quiet manner. This tells the reader he is a very quiet man.
Mr. Munson, head of a department of F & S, stomps out and sends in his resignation after dealing with Mrs. Barrows; others are fired, and others complain. This tells the reader Mrs. Barrows is arrogant and insensitive to others.

c. We find this quiet, conservative man is planning to murder Mrs. Barrows.

d. Mrs. Barrows is not really guilty of some hideous crime. Mr. Martin hates her because she has invaded his neat, private world.
He is threatened by her changes and feels his feelings of hate are justified. In fact, he places her on trial in his mind and decides her "crimes" are deserving of the death sentence. Her horrible crimes, however, are present only in his mind.

e. The point of view is third person limited omniscient because we are only told what Mr. Martin is thinking and planning. We see Mrs. Barrows from his point of view. Her thoughts are unknown to the reader. The story, however, is not written from first person because Mr. Martin is not the narrator, and the pronoun, *I*, is not used.

f. Answers will vary, but the following may be helpful:
Mr. Martin is a very quiet, strange man who is obsessed with his work. He has no sense of humor and hates any sort of change.

3.

c.

1) Mr. Martin enters the apartment.
2) He searches for something to use as a weapon.
3) He decides on a new plan.
4) He tells a series of lies to Mrs. Barrows about his plans to murder Fitweiler.
5) He exits the apartment and returns home.

These events are part of the rising action of the plot.

d. He figures out a way to get rid of Mrs. Barrows without murdering her.

4.

b. A climax is reached when Mrs. Barrows reports to Mr. Fitweiler about Mr. Martin's threats against his life.

c. Answers will vary.

d. The story does contain an element of irony in that Mrs. Barrows is in control of the office in the beginning of the story, but in the end the advantage is turned and Mr. Martin gets his way.

e. The business office is not just a building to Mr. Martin; it is a vital part of his life, so it is important to the story that this is where the conflict takes place.

f. All are flat. We only see one side to each character. All the things that Mr. Martin does which are unusual are out-of-character, even by his own admission, so he would still be classified as a flat character.

5.

a. "The Catbird Seat" is a good title for this story because it ends with a twist of irony that places a quiet, conservative Mr. Martin in a position where he controls what happens, rather than the flamboyant Mrs. Barrows, who thought she had everything under her control. It is interesting that Mr. Martin uses Mrs. Barrow's expression at the end to give her a hint of what would actually take place.

d.

1) D
2) B
3) C
4) E
5) A

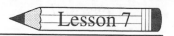

1. a. Read "To the Mountains" by Paul Horgan (pp. 423-453).

   b. Define the following words as used in the context of the story. The page number for each word is listed.

      1) petulant (p. 425)
      2) copious (p. 426)
      3) wraith (p. 437)

2. a. Look over Part One of "To the Mountains" (p. 423 to the break on p. 427). What sort of mood does the author set in Part One of the story?

   b. List at least five ways in which the story builds a sense of fear and dread for Julio and his family.

   c. Two words used in Part One of "To the Mountains" are not English words but Spanish with the following meanings:

      1) cañon - canyon
      2) piñón - pinyon; a pine seed

      What does the use of these words in the story tell you about the nationality of the characters?

3. a. Reread Part Two of "To the Mountains" (p. 427 to the break on p. 432).

   b. What method of characterization does the author use: direct, indirect, or both?

      Give reasons to support your answer.

   c. Who is the main character of the story?

   d. What sort of relationship do the two brothers share? What is the source of their conflict?

   e. Based on the first two parts of the story, write a brief character description of each of the two brothers, Luis and Julio.

4. a. Read Part Three of "To the Mountains" (p. 432 to the break on p. 436).

    b. What does their reaction to the waterfall indicate about the two brothers?

    c. Why do you think Julio kicked the cub's carcass off the ledge? How does this act change the mood of the day?

    d. At the end of the day Julio examines the gun and hands it back to his brother with a chuckle. How is this event an example of foreshadowing, and what is the author hinting might occur?

    e. The author, Paul Horgan, uses descriptive language to paint a picture of the mountains for the reader. Vivid language is used in his description of the eagle on pp. 434 - 435. Carefully read over this part of the story. Choose an animal and write a paragraph describing it. For example, you could choose to write about a rabbit leaping or a tiger stalking.

5. a. Reread Part Four of "To the Mountains" (p. 436 to the end of p. 439).

    b. What action did Julio take that was foreshadowed in Part Three?

    c. Why do you think Julio decided to begin this dangerous mission without his brother's knowledge or consent?

    d. What sort of struggle did Julio have within himself?

    e. Would you consider Julio a hero or a fool? Write a few paragraphs expressing your viewpoint on this issue. Provide examples from the story to support your viewpoint.

    f. Write a sentence using each of the following vocabulary words correctly: petulant, copious, wraith.

1.

b.

　1) petulant - ill-tempered,
　　annoying
　2) copious - large, abundant
　3) wraith - an apparition or ghost

2.

a. The author sets a mood of fear
　and desperation.

b. Possible answers:

　1) The husband left the family
　and won't return for a long time,
　leaving them without his care
　and protection.
　2) The mother has a newborn
　baby and is not well. This adds
　to the burden of the family.
　3) Josefina expresses that she
　will not be able to stay and help
　"forever" so she might leave any
　time.
　4) The family is poor with little
　food and clothing for warmth;
　and winter is coming.
　5) They live in an isolated area
　where there is little help
　available.
　6) The mother has doubts her
　husband will return home with
　the money and clothes they
　need.
　7) Josefina expresses doubts
　that they will make it through the
　winter.

c. The characters are of Spanish
　origin.

3.

b. The author uses both methods
　of characterization. The
　description given on p. 424 tells
　the reader the boys' ages and
　gives physical descriptions.
　However, you learn about each
　character's personality more
　from his conversations and
　actions.

c. The main character is Julio
　because the narrator focuses
　more on his perception of
　things.

d. The two brothers share a typical
　sibling relationship. They love
　each other and look out for one
　another, but they also disagree
　and argue between themselves.

　One of the main sources of
　conflict between them is the
　question of who is in a position
　of authority between them. Luis,
　being the oldest, feels he should
　be in a position of authority over
　his younger brother, but Julio
　resents his authority and feels
　he is old enough to take care of
　himself.

e. Answers will vary, but the
　following may be helpful:
　Luis is a stout boy of sixteen.
　The oldest of the two brothers,
　he is responsible and sensible.

　Julio is a slender, agile lad of
　thirteen. Although somewhat
　impulsive and reckless, he is
　kind-hearted and wants to do
　well for his family.

4.

b. Although they desire to do a man's job, they are still boys who look at this trip to the mountains as an adventure. This is evidenced by their desire to swim when they see the waterfall.

c. Although no explanation is given for why Julio kicked the cub's carcass, it seems that it could partially be the result of some feelings of jealousy because Luis has the idea of using it for bait.

Julio's act ends the day on a sour note, with both brothers being discouraged. His act had the effect of turning "happiness into misery" (p. 436).

d. Julio's examination of the gun, handing it back to Luis with a chuckle, and desire to surprise his brother hints that he has something planned that he will be doing secretly and his plan would involve the gun.

e. Answers will vary.

5.

b. Julio decided to take the gun and go on his own to kill a lion.

c. Julio wants to prove to his brother that he can do a man's job. He knows as long as he is with his brother he will only be allowed to assist him. He will not be allowed to shoot the gun or make any decisions. He also knows his brother would never consent to him going alone.

d. He struggled against feelings of fear, lonesomeness, and his own self doubt. In a way he was proving his manhood to himself as well as to Luis.

e. Different viewpoints will be expressed here. On one side, not only did Julio kill a mountain lion by himself with one shot, but he also skinned it. On the other hand, however, he placed the boys' mission in jeopardy by his foolish behavior. He left Luis and the horses without any protection or clue as to where he had gone or when he will be back.

f. Answers will vary.

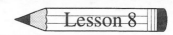
1. a. Reread Part Five of "To the Mountains" (p. 440 to the end of p. 441).

   b. What realization did Julio have concerning his brother?

   c. Read the third paragraph on p. 440. What is Julio's view towards animals?

   d. How is this different from the way many people view animals today? Do you agree or disagree with his view?

   e. Is there any Biblical basis to Julio's view? Explain. Give Scripture to support your answer.

   f. Julio wakes from his sleep to the sound of a bell, "like the bell of the church at home" (p. 441). Do you feel that God awakened him with the sound of a bell? What would have happened if Julio had fallen into a deep sleep in the cold snow?

   g. Have you ever had a time in your life when you felt God intervened in some way to keep you safe? Write a few paragraphs telling about the incident.

   h. Define the following words from the story:

      1) ingratiating (p. 444)
      2) mollifying (p. 444)
      3) penitent (p. 446)

2. a. Reread Part Six of "To the Mountains" (p. 442 to the break on p. 445).

   b. One of the conflicts in this story is the conflict between Luis and Julio. However, another conflict exists in the story that is very evident in Part Six. What would this conflict be?

   c. What does the lion carcass symbolize to Julio?

   d. What is signified by Julio dropping the carcass of the lion in order to run faster?

e. Write a few paragraphs explaining how Luis and Julio showed both maturity and immaturity in the situation with the wolf.

3. a. Reread Part Seven of "To the Mountains" (p. 445 to the break on p. 446).

    b. When did the climax of the conflict between man vs. nature take place?

    c. When did the climax of the conflict between the two brothers take place?

    d. After the brothers worked together to kill the wolf is there any change in the brothers' attitude toward one another? Give examples to support your answer.

    e. What was Luis's attitude toward Julio's foolish act when he confessed?

4. a. Reread Part Eight of "To the Mountains" (p. 446 to the break on p. 449).

    b. What is the point of view of this story? Give support for your answer from the story.

    c. How did Josefina react to Father Antonio's coming? Did Rosa have a different reaction?

    d. Contrast the reactions of Josefina and Rosa to the presence of Father Antonio.

    e. Does Father Antonio understand why the boys went to the mountains? How does he explain it to the women?

    f. Father Antonio asks the women, "How will a man ever know what goes on unless he goes out and looks at it?" Write a paragraph explaining what you feel he meant by this question.

a. Reread Part Nine of "To the Mountains" (p. 449 to the break on p. 452).

b. In the second paragraph on p. 449 the author again describes the beauty of the mountains. How has the setting contributed to shape this story?

c. How does the priest's presence help Rosa?

d. Why does Josefina stay after she is no longer needed? What does this tell you about her?

e. What does Father Antonio see in Julio that hints at the change that has taken place? What does his mother realize?

f. In this story all conflicts and fears are resolved favorably. The author skillfully manipulated us, built a sense of dread, then delivered a good conclusion. Julio's behavior can be described as rebellious. He takes unwise risks in an attempt to prove himself mature. Although it turned out for the best, Julio jeopardized the welfare of the rest of the family.

g. Think of an instance in your life when you acted unwisely, assuming more responsibility than you should have. Write a paragraph describing the incident and any lessons learned by it. Write a second paragraph describing a situation in which you acted appropriately, pointing out the reasons for the decision you made. Conclude by describing the safeguards existing in your life which enable you to make wise decisions and to learn from poor ones. As you consider topics for these paragraphs, don't feel limited to major events. Meaningful lessons can be learned from minor episodes.

h. Reread Part Ten of "To the Mountains" (pp. 452 to 453).

i. Why did Father Antonio choose not to tell the brothers' story for them in the letter to their father? What did he tell their father?

j. Do you feel you have matured in your Christian walk as a result of the incidents you experienced? Why or why not?

k. Write a friendly letter to a parent, friend, or relative telling how God is working in your life to help you to become a mature Christian. Follow the format for a friendly letter. Whether or not you mail the letter is up to you. Be sure to watch your comma placement.

> *(heading)*
> 123 Main Street
> Jacksonville, Florida 32044
> October 24, 1999
>
> Dear Aunt Sue, *(salutation or greeting)*
>
> *(Indent)* _____
>
> _____*(Body)*_____
>
> _____
>
> _____
>
> _____
>
> _____
>
>   With love, *(closing)*
>
>   Sandy *(signature)*

l. Complete the following sentences with the correct vocabulary word: ingratiating, mollifying, penitent.

1) The soft music transformed the frustrated customer, _____ his anger.

2) The young girl waited on the couple attentively, _____ herself to them.

3) Her friend was _____ about the problems her behavior had caused.

b. He left his brother without any protection. Only now, after he accomplished what he set out to do, is his vision unclouded to see the possible consequences of his actions.

c. Julio believes it is his place to conquer the animals as well as to love them. He feels the animals were placed here on the earth to serve him.

d. Many people today tend to regard animals as equals and believe man is wrong to kill, capture, or use animals in any way that does not benefit the animal.

Views on agreement or disagreement will vary.

e. The Bible states that man is to dominate animals and gives support to the fact that mankind is to use them for the purpose of food and clothing.

Supporting Scriptures:
Gen. 1:28b - "... rule over the fish of the sea and over the birds of the sky, and over every living thing that moves on the earth."

Gen. 3:21 (KJV) - "Unto Adam also and to his wife did the Lord God make coats of skins and clothe them."

Lev. 11:2b (KJV) - "... These are the beasts which ye shall eat among all the beasts that are on the earth."

f. We can only speculate that God woke Julio with the sound of a bell.

If Julio had continued sleeping, he might have frozen to death.

g. Answers will vary.

h.
1) ingratiating - to make oneself acceptable; to obtain another's good favor by conscious effort
2) mollifying - to pacify or calm another's anger or distress
3) penitent - being sorry for one's misdeeds

2.
b. The conflict is man vs. nature as is evidenced by the brothers' battle with the wolf.

c. The prize of the carcass represented proof of Julio's manhood.

d. The fact that he dropped it in order to run faster shows the reader that it no longer held that value to him in light of the knowledge that he could be the cause of his brother being harmed.

Supporting statement: "All his greatness of accomplishment disappeared. What good was this smelling and frozen catskin now?"
(p. 442)

49

2.

e. Luis demonstrated his maturity by staying calm and handling the situation in a logical, sensible way. He kept his voice steady and told his brother exactly what to do without becoming emotional or angry. However, he showed his immaturity by being impatient and attacking the wolf with a knife while it was wounded instead of letting his brother kill it completely with the gun.

Julio demonstrated his maturity by staying calm in a difficult situation, listening to his brother's instructions, and being cautious about approaching the wounded wolf. He showed his immaturity by the way he rushed into the camp in a panic without being cautious.

3.

b. The climax of the conflict between man vs. nature took place when they killed the wolf, therefore conquering nature and its threat to them.

c. The climax of the conflict between the two brothers, man vs. man, took place at the same time. They worked together to kill the wolf instead of quarreling amongst themselves.

d. There is a definite change in the brothers' attitude toward one another. Julio has come to accept his brother's authority as is evidenced by the fact that he asks Luis where to stab the wolf. Luis realizes his rescue is due to Julio's skill as a marksman and recognizes that Julio has matured as a result of his experience. He now accepts him as more of an equal. The brothers begin to work together as a team to accomplish their mission.

e. Again Luis shows his maturity by forgiving Julio and realizing that "the terrors of experience were more useful to his young brother than any rebuke" (p. 446).

4.

b. The point of view is third person omniscient.

The author freely gives us information about the characters and their circumstances that are far beyond the perceptions of the characters themselves.

c. Josefina displays a lack of enthusiasm at the priest coming to visit, and even seems somewhat annoyed. Rosa, however, is joyful and at peace.

d. The women react differently to the presence of the priest because Josefina liked being the person in charge and is "… furious at his kind of power over and against women" (p. 447). She obviously does not want anyone to have authority over her. Rosa, on the other hand, welcomes his authority and feels with his coming "… that she need have no further fear" (p. 447).

e. Father Antonio seems to understand why the boys went into the mountains.

He tells the women that next to the challenge of "catching a sinner and taking away his sin" he loves the challenges offered by the mountains, catching fish from the streams and trapping the beaver. In the same way the boys went to experience these challenges.

Answers will vary, but the following may be helpful:
He was trying to explain to the women that the boys will never become men and understand the world around them unless they go out into the world alone and experience its challenges.

. The setting, although beautiful, is also a harsh place to survive and make a living. This helps to establish the conflict of man vs. nature.

. Under his authority and with his encouragement she is able to regain her strength, both physical and mental, and again take over the household tasks.

. She stays with the hope that she will be the godmother of the child. Being godmother is important enough to her that she stays even after she is needed.

This act tells you that she is a person who craves recognition and possibly even some sort of family connection.

e. Father Antonio sees that Julio stands taller, has a "nobility of bearing" in his shoulders (p. 452), and is curiously contented with the fact that they have furs to keep their little sister warm.

Julio's mother realizes that "he had gone and conquered the wilderness that was his brother's by birth" (p. 452).

g. Answers will vary.

i. He felt that the father needed to hear the story from the brothers' own lips.

He merely let the father know in his letter that they had become men.

j. Allow for discussion.

l.
1) mollifying
2) ingratiating
3) penitent

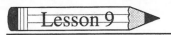
1. a. Read "Young Goodman Brown" (pp. 53-68).

   b. Nathaniel Hawthorne is one of the finest authors in America history. His novel, *The Scarlet Letter*, is often rated among five best American novels, and his short stories are regarded some of the world's treasures.

   c. To help you gain further insight into the author's viewpoint, is helpful to know that Hawthorne had a great interest in colonial history, especially that of the Puritans. In fact, man of his characters are Puritans or people with Puritan beliefs and characteristics. Often he interwove into his stories som of his own family's history from that time period. For example, in "Young Goodman Brown," the devil tells Goodman Brown that his grandfather "lashed a Quaker woman so smartly through the streets of Salem" (p. 56). In truth, it was recorded that one of Hawthorne's ancestors gav orders that Quakers should be whipped in the streets.

   d. What is the setting of this story? What is the time period?

   e. In your own words tell your teacher a brief summary of the literal events of the story.

   f. Define the following words as used in the context of the stor

      1) ecclesiastical (p. 60)
      2) venerable (p. 64)
      3) proselytes (p. 65)

2. a. Reread the story from page 53 until you reach the middle c page 57. Stop before the paragraph beginning, "As he spoke. . ."

   b. Nathaniel Hawthorne is known for his excellent use of allegory. An **allegory** is a story that has a double meaning, one literal and the other figurative. In an allegory, characte things, places, and actions often have symbolic meanings. Also, the story usually portrays a moral truth or lesson.

c. When trying to unravel the meaning of an allegory, it is important to pay attention to the parts of the story which might have a double meaning. For example, Faith is not only the name of Goodman Brown's wife; she is also a symbol for his faith in God. In the story there is a parallel between Goodman Brown leaving his wife, Faith, and leaving behind his faith in God.

d. Look through pp. 53-57, and try to find other people, objects, places, or actions which have symbolic meaning. Make a list of words and phrases that may have another meaning and decide what you think each symbolizes.
Example: Faith - faith in God

e. What does the color of the symbolic hair ribbons tell the reader about Faith?

f. What does the word *justified* mean in the context of the paragraph beginning "With this excellent resolve ..." (p. 54)?

g. At the bottom of page 55, Goodman Brown threatens to return. What does the devil use to persuade him to go further?

a. Reread the rest of page 57 to page 62, stopping before the paragraph that begins, "Ha! ha! ha!"

b. How do the devil's revelations concerning Goody Cloyse, Deacon Gookin, and the minister affect Goodman Brown?

c. On page 59, Goodman Brown swears he won't take another step. In the next paragraph, beginning "You will think ..." is another step in his loss of faith. What is it?

d. On page 62, Goodman Brown expresses "My Faith is gone!" What reaction does he have to losing his faith?

e. Notice that throughout the story the author uses language that was used in that area during the time period of the story setting. When an author uses language and expressions that are peculiar to a certain group of people, the story is said to contain **dialect**. Locate and write ten words or phrases that reflect dialect in the story. Decide how we would express the same idea today and write those words opposite the dialect words. Use a dictionary to help you with any difficult words. Example: Methought - I thought (p. 54)

4. a. Reread the final part of the story (pp. 62 to 68).

   b. The theme of the story is revealed by the character of the devil on two different occasions when he speaks of "the communion of your race" (pp. 65 and 66). What is the theme the author is revealing here?

   c. What is the conflict in this story?

   d. In a few sentences explain the allegory of this story.

   e. What major flaw do you see in Goodman Brown's character?

   f. How did this contribute to his loss of faith?

   g. Good examples of allegories are the parables of the Bible. Which parable do you feel would best describe Goodman Brown's character?

   h. Write a paragraph describing this parable and tell why it best fits Goodman Brown's character.

5. a. Throughout this story, the author uses conditional words such as *appeared*, *seemed*, and *like*. Do you think what Goodman Brown experienced was a dream or reality? Is it important to the meaning of the story for you to determine whether it is a dream or reality?

   b. What was the result of this experience in the life of Goodman Brown? How did it change him?

c. Hawthorne was obviously skeptical of the validity of the Christian experience. He viewed it in the same manner as Goodman Brown, with distrust. The problem of sin was often addressed in his various writings. What essential elements of the Christian experience did he fail to understand?

Prepare some Scriptures and personal testimony that you would share with Hawthorne if you had a chance.

Discuss your presentation with your teacher and share it with a family member or friend.

d. Read the following sentences. Using a thesaurus, complete each sentence with a synonym for the word in parenthesis.

1) He wore his _____ (ecclesiastical) robe for the ceremony.
2) The _____ (venerable) position of chairman was changed with the ceremonial transfer of the gavel.
3) The Christian _____ (proselytes) waited for the baptism to begin.

e. Optional: Read *Pilgrim's Progress* by John Bunyan. This is also an allegory. Compare the two stories. What is the moral lesson of each?

f. How does *Pilgrim's Progress* differ from "Young Goodman Brown"?

What does this tell you about each author?

1.

d. The setting is colonial America during the time the Puritans were dominant in American society.

The approximate time is during the seventeenth century.

e. Goodman Brown leaves his house one evening and goes to the edge of the forest where he has an appointment with the devil. They take a path through the wood where Goodman Brown eventually attends a black mass and commits his soul to the devil. The next morning, he awakes at the edge of the forest and wonders whether or not his experience was real. He remains skeptical of people and their appearances for the rest of his life.

f.

1) ecclesiastical - in reference to someone or something that is affiliated with a church
2) venerable - worthy of respect
3) proselytes - religious converts

2.

d. Answers will vary, but the following may be helpful:
elder traveler - Satan
snake staff - evil and deception
pink ribbons - pink is a combination of red and white - the red symbolizes sinfulness and the white symbolizes purity
forest - sin and unbelief

e. Pink is the combination of red and white with red symbolizing sinfulness and white symbolizing purity. The ribbons show the reader Faith's own imperfection and sin combined with goodness. Clearly, if the virtuous Faith is tainted, then no one is safe from flaw and blemish.

f. *Justified* means to prove actions to be right or just. In the context of this story Goodman Brown feels he is justified in continuing his journey because of his resolve to never leave Faith again after this night. He is rationalizing his wrong behavior.

g. First he tells Goodman Brown to keep walking with him, using the argument that if he is unable to persuade him, he can always turn back. Then the devil reasons with him as to why he should continue his journey, explaining away his faith. He asks Goodman why he should fight temptation when all the members of his family and respectable people he knows have given into temptation in the past. One of Satan's favorite arguments is to point out the sin of others and tell us, "See, they did it, and it didn't hurt them."

3.

b. His revelations shake the faith of Goodman Brown further. These are people whom he has admired and looked to for guidance. Finding their outward appearance to be different than their true nature makes him unsure of anything he has believed in the past.

c. The devil tells Goodman Brown "when you feel like moving again." The next move will be Goodman Brown's own choice, without any help from the devil.

d. With his faith gone, Goodman Brown sinks into a state of despair. He believes all to be evil and no longer has the will to fight the devil. "Come, devil; for to thee is this world given" (p. 62).

e.
prithee - please (p. 53)
afeard - afraid (p. 53)
tarry - wait (p. 53)
dost - do (p. 53)
'twixt - between (p. 53)
thy - your (p. 54)
't would - it would (p. 54)
agone - ago (p. 55)
wholly - completely (p. 55)
whence - from where (p. 55)
wot'st of - know of (p. 55)
thither - there (p. 55)
sayest - say (p. 55)
thee - you (p. 55)
thou - you (p. 55)
wouldst - would (p. 56)
fain - gladly (p. 56)
howbeit - however (p. 56)
husbandman - farmer (p. 56)
whither - where (p. 57)
betake - take (p. 57)
forsooth - no doubt (p. 58)
bane - deadly poison (p. 58)
thus - in this manner (p. 59)
amidst - amid (p. 59)
deemed - thought or believed (p. 59)
athwart - across (p. 60)
durst - dare (p. 60)
goodly - attractive (p. 60)

spur up - hurry (p. 60)
aught - anything (p. 61)
espy - catch sight of (p. 64)
ye - you (p. 65)
lo - see (p. 66)

4.
b. Basically, the theme of the story is that even though mankind appears good, it is basically evil.

c. The conflict in the story is man vs. himself. Goodman Brown is dealing with his own doubts. Although Satan has a part in the introduction of doubt, the conflict occurs within the character of Goodman Brown.

d. The allegory is progressive loss of faith. The path through the woods represents the progressive stages of doubt leading to unbelief and renunciation of one's faith.

e. Goodman Brown is unable to accept any evil in anyone. He conveniently seems to pass judgment on others without looking inward.

f. When he finds fault in others, he doubts that his faith is real. He eventually succumbs to his feelings of doubt and abandons his faith completely.

g. The parable of the speck and the log (Matthew 7:1-5) would best describe Goodman Brown's character because it speaks about judging others.

4.

h. Answers will vary, but the following may be helpful: The parable tells us to be careful we are not looking at the speck, which represents a small sin, in our brother's eye and pay no attention to the log, which represents a large amount of sin, in our own eye. Just as the allegory in the parable represents the idea of judging others wrongfully, Goodman Brown was looking at the fault in the lives of others without realizing that his own life contained fault.

5.

a. It is strictly a matter of opinion as to whether the reader thinks Goodman Brown was having a dream or it was reality.

The result of the experience is the same either way.

b. He did not change his life to become an evil sinner, but he did change his attitude.

He no longer trusted people or God. He viewed everyone with suspicion and contempt, including his own wife.

c. The essential elements Hawthorne failed to understand were the elements of grace and forgiveness. All of us sin, but we have forgiveness through Jesus Christ.

Suggested supportive Scriptures:
Romans 3:23 - "... for all have sinned and fall short of the glory of God ..."

Ephesians 2:8 - "For by grace you have been saved through faith; and that not of yourselves, it is the gift of God ..."
I John 1:9 - "If we confess our sins, He is faithful and righteous to forgive us our sins and to cleanse us from all unrighteousness."

d.
1) religious, clerical
2) honored, respected
3) converts, disciple
    As long as the meaning remains the same, other words may also be used.

e. The moral lesson of *Pilgrim's Progress* is that sin can be conquered through faith in God. The moral lesson in "Young Goodman Brown" is that man is basically evil with no hope of redemption.

f. *Pilgrim's Progress* is a moral lesson that gives us hope for mankind while the lesson of "Young Goodman Brown" is that there is no hope for mankind.

It is obvious that the author of *Pilgrim's Progress* is a Christian and has a view of the world that includes God's grace and forgiveness towards mankind. Hawthorne, however, was obviously skeptical of Christianity; therefore, he portrays mankind as lost without hope.

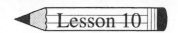
1. a. Read "The Fall of the House of Usher" (pp. 69-91).

   b. Edgar Allan Poe is often considered to be the father of the American short story as his style influenced so many other authors. He believed the purpose of literature was "to amuse by arousing thought," and "The Fall of the House of Usher" is one of his great masterpieces of literature that fits this description.

   c. The **exposition** part of the plot is used by the author to provide the reader with the background information needed to understand the rest of the story. What background information does Poe provide the reader in this part of the story?

   d. Poe has the ability to paint a picture with words. He does this through the use of imagery. **Imagery** is a literary device used by an author to create a picture in the mind of the reader through the use of descriptive words and phrases. Sketch a drawing of how you think the House of Usher would look according to Poe's description.

   e. What is the significance of the house being called "The House of Usher"?

   f. Poe uses complex vocabulary throughout the story, so keep your dictionary handy to look up words. Define the following words.

      1) appellation (p. 71)
      2) phantasmagoric (p. 73)
      3) hypochondriac (p. 78)

2. a. Reread "The Fall of the House of Usher" from the bottom of page 73 up to the paragraph on page 77 which begins "For several days ensuing …"

   b. How does the author describe Roderick Usher? Does he use the direct or indirect method for his description?

   c. From what point of view is the story written?

> *Teacher Note:* Although Edgar Allan Poe is a controversial author, no study of American literature would be complete without including a selection of his writing. Please use this lesson at your discretion.

d. Poe's stories are known for their unity of mood. In fact, because of this unity and his use of classical form, Edgar Allan Poe is probably one of the best known American writers abroad. This classical style of literature, based on the style of literature developed in ancient Greece, has the effect of simplicity, balance, and controlled emotion. What mood is Poe creating in this story?

e. Find examples in the story that Poe uses to consistently create this mood.

f. Some people see a glass as half full, and others see it as half empty; it all depends on your point of view. Rewrite the paragraph on page 73 that begins with "The room in which …" and change the mood from one of darkness and dread to a mood of cheerfulness. Do not change the room itself; change only the point of view from which the room is described.

3. a. Reread "The Fall of the House of Usher" from page 77 and stop on page 84 with the paragraph that begins, "It was, especially …"

b. What extraordinary talents does Roderick Usher possess?

c. How does the narrator's description of Usher's expressions of art and music help us to better understand the character of Roderick Usher?

d. What is the reader told of the character of Madeline and her relationship with her brother?

e. How does Madeline's death affect the mental state of Roderick Usher?

f. What reason does Roderick give for keeping the body of Madeline in the vaults of the house for a fortnight (two weeks)?

g. Roderick Usher expresses his feelings and personality through art and music. Using magazine pictures, family pictures, and perhaps even small objects, create a collage that expresses your personality.

4. a. Reread "The Fall of the House of Usher" from page 84 to the end of the story.

   b. What is the climax of this story?

   c. Having finished the story, go back to pp. 83 and 84 of the story. What hints does Poe give the reader about the climax of the story?

      What is this literary technique called?

   d. How does the author increase the feelings of suspense in the rising action part of the story?

   e. How does the narrator's mental condition weaken?

   f. Is there any connection between this and the mental condition of Roderick Usher? Support your answer.

   g. How does the narrator escape ruin and death?

   h. Poe is known for his ability to create a feeling of suspense in his stories. Write a few paragraphs describing a situation and create a feeling of suspense. For example, describe a cat stalking a mouse or a person climbing to the top of a mountain.

5. a. Poe gives detailed descriptions of the house and Roderick Usher throughout the story. What relationship exists between the two?

   b. In many ways the house and Roderick Usher are alike. Compare the author's description of the house to the person of Roderick Usher.

   c. Roderick Usher's fears and anxieties made him a prisoner in his own home. He tells the narrator that he has not left the house for years (p. 76). What other evidence does the author give of his mental imprisonment?

d. Poe's "The Fall of the House of Usher" and Hawthorne's "Young Goodman Brown" are similar in the mood they create and use of imagery, but the outcomes and reality of the events are very different. Explain the difference between the two stories.

e. This story ends with a sad and rather twisted turn of events. If you were the author, would you have given the story a different ending? Write a few paragraphs giving a different conclusion to this story. Be sure to use descriptive language to keep consistent with the author's style of writing.

f. Use the correct vocabulary word to complete the following sentences: appellation, phantasmagoric, hypochondriac.

   1) He is also known by the _____, Sir Edward Simon.
   2) They became convinced he was a _____ because he took off many days due to illness.
   3) The images were so _____ that he was not convinced that what he was seeing was real.

1.

c. He gives information concerning the family background, his friend's illness, and the origin of their relationship.

e. The house did not belong to any one particular branch of the Usher family; therefore, the name represented the merger of the title of the property to all the family of Usher.

f.

1) appellation - a name or title
2) phantasmagoric - a rapidly changing series of objects - real or imagined
3) hypochondriac - a person who is convinced he is ill when actually he is not

2.

b. The author describes him as being pale with large eyes, possessing thin lips, prominent nose, and a distinct chin. His appearance is rather unkempt, and his personality is depressed and unstable (p. 74).

The author uses the indirect method to describe the character of Roderick Usher.

c. The story is written in the first person point of view.

d. The mood created in the story is one of depression, darkness, and dread. Poe uses the description of the home, the emotions of the narrator, and his description of the characters to create this mood.

e. Many examples can be used to show how Poe creates this mood. Some of the examples are:
1) dull, dark, and soundless day (p. 69)
2) bleak walls, upon vacant eye-like windows (p. 69)
3) There was an iciness, a sinking, sickening of the heart...(p. 69)
4) an atmosphere which had no affinity with the air of heaven, but which had reeked up from the decayed trees. . . (p. 72)
5) The now ghostly pallor of the skin, and now miraculous luster of the eye, above all things startled and even awed me (p. 74).
6) "I must abandon life and reason together, in some struggle with the grim phantasm, FEAR" (p. 76).

f. Answers will vary. An example follows:
The room in which I found myself was very large and lofty. The majestic windows were long, narrow, and pointed and let in the bright sunlight that exposed the beautiful oaken floor and the prominent objects around the room. As I looked about the room, the light revealed a graceful vaulted and fretted ceiling. Rich draperies hung upon the walls. An abundance of lavish antique furniture was distributed throughout the room and many handsome books and exquisite musical instruments lay scattered about, giving the room

an air of sophistication. I felt that I breathed an atmosphere of delightful satisfaction. An air of anticipation penetrated throughout the room.

3.

b. Roderick Usher has the ability to express his ideas on canvas. "If ever mortal painted an idea, that mortal was Roderick Usher" (p. 78). Also, he possesses the ability to write lyrics and play music which are "the result of that intense mental collectedness and concentration ..." (p. 79).

c. Roderick Usher is able to express his feelings and fears best through his art and music, and therefore, the narrator's descriptions give the reader insight into the character of Roderick Usher. For example, the verses of the song which appear on pp. 79-81 show us Usher's feelings of how happier days have now given way to evil and sorrow.

d. The reader is told that Madeline is Roderick's twin (p. 83), that she is a beloved sister and his sole companion for long years, his last and only relative on earth (p. 76), and that she suffers with an unknown disease that is killing her (p. 77). The only hint the reader has of Madeline's personality is the fact that she is quiet and does not complain. "... she had steadily borne up against the pressure of her malady and had not betaken herself finally to bed ..." (p. 77).

e. Roderick Usher becomes more

mentally unstable. He neglects his other activities, roams around aimlessly, his voice shakes, and he stares vacantly for hours (p. 84).

f. He fears that because of the peculiar nature of his sister's disease that certain medical men may remove the body for observation if it is buried in the open family cemetery.

4.

b. The climax occurs when Madeline appears and falls upon her brother, killing him.

c.

1) "the mockery of a faint blush upon the bosom and the face" (p. 83) - hints that the sister is not really dead

2) "the luminousness of his eye had utterly gone out" (p. 84) - hints that Roderick is going to die

3) "listening to some imaginary sound" (p. 84) - hints at the sister's escape from her tomb

4) "struggled to reason off the nervousness which had dominion over me" (p. 84) - the narrator's nervousness hints that something dreadful is about to happen

This technique is called foreshadowing.

d. The night is stormy, Roderick is becoming more mentally unstable, and the narrator reads to him the novel, *Mad Trist*, which is describing sounds similar to what they are actually hearing. This all works together to increase the reader's feeling of suspense.

The narrator's mental condition weakens in that he becomes inexplicably nervous and unable to sleep.

His nervousness turns to alarm and then fear, behavior similar to Roderick at the beginning of the story.

His mental condition is affected by his exposure to Roderick. "It was no wonder that his condition terrified - that it infected me" (p. 84).

The narrator flees the house when Madeline appears, thus barely escaping with his sanity and his life.

The house and Roderick Usher are mirror images of each other.

The house compares to Roderick Usher in the following ways:

1) Just as Roderick Usher isolates himself from the outside world, the house possesses an air of isolation. It is situated in an isolated tract of country; it has "bleak walls," "vacant eye-like windows" (p.69), and is enshrouded in a gaseous vapor (p.86).

2) The crumbling, degenerate state of the house is similar to Roderick Usher's crumbling sanity.

3) When Madeline falls upon Roderick, killing him, the house also crumbles and falls, as if the life of the last of the line of Ushers was the very crumbling mortar holding the aged stones in place.

c. In Roderick's poem, "The Haunted Palace," he makes reference to the "old time entombed" (p. 80), that lets the reader know he is feeling that he is the last of his old family and is now entombed in the rotting house. Also, he paints a long tunnel or vault which seems to be buried deep in the heart of the earth with no outlet for escape. This conveys to the reader his feelings of hopeless confinement.

d. "Young Goodman Brown" allows the reader to question the validity of the events of the story while "The Fall of the House of Usher" leaves the reader no choice but to accept all the narrator describes as having actually happened. Hawthorne's story is filled with vague suggestions of events and conditional words like "perhaps" and "possibly." Poe incorporates none of this uncertainty in his story.

e. Answers will vary.

f.
1) appellation
2) hypochondriac
3) phantasmagoric

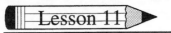
1. a. Read "Bartleby the Scrivener" by Herman Melville (pp. 92-135).

2. a. "Bartleby the Scrivener" is a short story written by Herman Melville, a nineteenth century author. Herman Melville is famous as the author of a great American novel. Do you know what novel he wrote?

   b. Reread pp. 92-99 of "Bartleby the Scrivener." From which point of view is this story written?

   c. Who is the narrator of the story?

   d. What is a scrivener? How many scriveners does the narrator have working for him and what are their names? What was Ginger Nut's position?

   e. Does the author use the direct or indirect method to describe the characters in the story?

   f. Using the detailed information given, write a brief description of each of the characters whom the author has introduced with the exception of Bartleby.

   g. Using a thesaurus, write two synonyms for each of the following words from the story:

      1) waive (p. 92)
      2) arduous (p. 93)
      3) ignominiously (p. 103)

3. a. Reread "Bartleby the Scrivener" beginning on page 100 and ending with the last paragraph on page 109.

   b. What method does the author use to describe Bartleby's personality to the reader?

   c. What sort of activities does Bartleby "prefer not" to participate in?

   d. When Bartleby first "prefers not" to do something, why does the narrator turn and ask the opinions of the other workers?

e. On page 109 the narrator gives reasons why he decides to tolerate Bartleby's peculiar behavior. What are these reasons?

f. Write a brief description of the character of Bartleby.

a. Melville's first works were travel-adventure novels written in the romantic style that was popular in the mid-nineteenth century. His style changed, however, under the influence of Nathaniel Hawthorne, to become more filled with examinations of life's deeper meanings, double meanings, and symbolism. The story, "Bartleby the Scrivener," is one of a collection of short stories and prose written in this manner by Melville called *The Piazza Tales*. What style of writing does Melville use in this story?

b. Describe the on-and-off "good, natural arrangement" between Nippers and Turkey. What do you think is the principle cause for this bizarre fluctuation in personality and performance?

c. Describe the setting of the office in which the story is set. What sort of mood is created by this setting?

d. What effect does this atmosphere seem to have on Bartleby?

e. Some people are greatly affected by their surroundings or even by the type of weather outside. Think of a situation in which you were affected by your surroundings. Write a few paragraphs telling how your surroundings affected you.

5. a. Reread pp. 110-119 of "Bartleby the Scrivener."

b. What discovery does the narrator make concerning Bartleby's living arrangements?

c. After looking through Bartleby's desk, and discovering he is living in the office, what conclusion does the narrator come to concerning Bartleby's mental state? Support your answer with a quote from the story.

d. How does the narrator deal with his discovery?

e. When the narrator reaches the point of frustration that cause him to want to dismiss Bartleby, the narrator tells us that, "I strangely felt something superstitious knocking at my heart, forbidding me to carry out my purpose, and denouncing me for a villain if I dared to breathe one bitter word against this forlornest of mankind" (p. 115). What do you feel the superstitious knocking represents?

f. What decision does Bartleby announce to the narrator in this portion of the story?

g. What reason does Bartleby give for his refusal to work?

h. The narrator decides that Bartleby's eyes are causing him problems and that is the reason for Bartleby's decision not to work. Do you feel that is what Bartleby meant by his question?

i. What is the narrator's reaction to Bartleby's announcement that he has "given up copying"?

j. The narrator tells the reader that "my vanity got the better of my pity" (p. 119). What does this statement tell you about the narrator's personality?

k. Write a sentence using each of the following vocabulary words correctly.

   1) waive (p. 92)
   2) arduous (p. 93)
   3) ignominiously (p. 103)

2
a. Herman Melville wrote *Moby Dick.*

b. The story is written from first person point of view.

c. The narrator is a lawyer who has the position of Master in Chancery in the state of New York. The author does not give his name.

d. A scrivener is a person who copies law documents.

The narrator has two scriveners working for him, Turkey and Nippers.

Ginger Nut is an errand boy.

e. The author uses the indirect method.

f. Narrator: an elderly lawyer who is fairly unambitious. He is modest, prudent, and patient.

Turkey: a short, plump, elderly, somewhat sloppily-dressed Englishman. He is described as having two different personalities. In the morning he is a steady-handed, diligent worker; however, in the afternoon he becomes rather hot-tempered and reckless.

Nippers: a young man about 25 years old. He is whiskered with a yellowish complexion, which makes him look somewhat like a pirate. He is neatly dressed and rather nervous. He suffers from indigestion which makes him irritable. His irritability and nervousness are apparent mainly in the morning; in the afternoon, he grows calmer and becomes a good worker.

Ginger Nut: a young boy, twelve years old. He is a quick-witted errand boy.

g.
1) waive - relinquish, abandon, surrender
2) arduous - demanding, difficult, grueling
3) ignominiously - disgracefully, shamefully, scornfully

3.
b. The author reveals Bartleby's personality using the indirect method. The reader learns about his personality from his reactions and comments to the narrator and other members of the office staff.

c. He doesn't like to check documents by reading them over with another person, run errands, or relay messages to another employee. Bartleby does not participate in any activity that requires him to interact with other people.

d. The narrator has a weak personality and looks for approval and agreement before he takes any action.

e. He tolerates Bartleby's behavior because he is useful to him. He is a good worker, quiet, always available, and trustworthy. Also, his weak personality would rather tolerate Bartleby than take the action necessary to dismiss him.

3.

f. Bartleby is quiet, neat, calm, industrious, and trustworthy. He is, however, stubborn in his decisions. Also, his responses to others are so mechanical that he seems devoid of any emotion. He is existing in his own little world and refuses to let others affect it in any way that he does not desire.

4.

a. The story is an allegory and uses realism.

b. Nippers is irritable in the mornings due to indigestion. Turkey flies into fits of rage in the afternoons. Apparently, alcohol has opposite effects on Nippers and Turkey. Both probably enjoy a few drinks at lunch. This seems to calm Nippers' indigestion, but causes Turkey to become high-strung. On p. 107 Turkey explains Nippers' change of heart in the afternoon by saying, "All beer, gentleness is effects of beer."

c. The office is described as having a view that either "looked upon the white wall of the interior of a spacious sky-light shaft" (p.94) or "a lofty brick wall, black by age" (p.94). It is tightly closed in by other buildings. The interior of the office is divided into one area for the narrator and the other area containing desks for the scriveners. Bartleby is closed off from the other employees by a high, green folding screen. The work is described as " a very dull, wearisome, and lethargic affair."

The setting creates a rather depressing and isolated atmosphere.

d. The atmosphere seems to affec Bartleby to do his work "silently palely, and mechanically," fitting into the rather depressing and isolated atmosphere created at the office.

e. Answers will vary.

5.

b. He discovers that Bartleby is living in the office.

c. He comes to the conclusion tha Bartleby is mentally unstable. "What I saw that morning persuaded me that the scrivene was the victim of innate and incurable disorder. I might give alms to his body; but his body did not pain him; it was his sou that suffered, and his soul I could not reach."

d. He calls Bartleby into his office with the purpose of finding out more about him. However, whe he gets no answers to satisfy h curiosity, he becomes again frustrated with the situation an his inability to find a solution.

e. The superstitious knocking represents his conscience letting him know that he shoulc have compassion on Bartleby and not let his own frustration and desires cause Bartleby harm.

f. Bartleby announces that he has decided upon doing no more writing.

j. When the narrator questions him as to why he refuses to copy, Bartleby only answers with the question, "Do you not see the reason for yourself?"

i. The narrator notices Bartleby's eyes are "dull and glazed" and assumes there is a physical reason for the refusal to work. However, Bartleby's dull, glazed look comes from more of an internal problem with his mental state of health. Bartleby is asking the narrator whether he can see that he is depressed and having mental problems.

. The narrator decides that "he had now become a millstone" (p. 118) and that he must dismiss him.

. The statement tells us that although he pities Bartleby, his own self-interests are the priority in his life. He was kind to Bartleby because he saw himself as a bestower of mercy upon unfortunate souls such as Bartleby, but ultimately the narrator decides Bartleby is of no further use to him and dismisses him, congratulating himself on being a good manager of the situation.

k. Answers will vary.

1. a. Reread pp. 119-122.

   b. How does Bartleby's refusal to leave affect the narrator?

   c. What is the conflict in this story? How would you classify the conflict?

   d. How does the writer build the suspense in the story?

   e. From this section of the story give one example that shows how the internal conflict is increasing in the narrator.

   f. Do some research about mental illness. What are its causes, how is it manifested, and how is it treated? Discuss your findings with your teacher. What do you feel would be the best way to handle the situation with Bartleby?

2. a. Reread pp.123-127.

   b. The narrator quotes the Scripture, "A new commandment give I unto you, that ye love one another" (I John 2:8). How does this Scripture relate to his relationship with Bartleby?

   c. At one point the narrator decides it is his responsibility to take care of Bartleby, to let him have his space in the office, help him all he can, and bother him no further. However, his decision is changed. What causes him to change his mind?

   d. How does the narrator decide to remedy his situation?

   e. How does Bartleby react to the narrator's move?

   f. What hints are given to you by the writer that the narrator is fighting an internal struggle with his conscience?

3. a. Reread pp. 128-131.

 b. What happens to Bartleby when the narrator vacates the office?

 c. Why does the narrator agree to talk with Bartleby at the landlord's urging?

 d. Why is Bartleby uncharacteristically wordy in his meeting with the narrator on the stairs of the old office?

 e. Often Bartleby is described as quietly standing facing a wall. He did this in the office, and again at Tombs. What symbolic meaning does the wall have in this story?

4. a. Reread pp. 132-135.

 b. Why is Bartleby angry with the narrator and refuses to talk with him when he comes to Tombs to visit?

 c. When Mr. Cutlets approaches Bartleby about having dinner with him, Bartleby replies that "I am unused to dinners." What sort of food did Bartleby eat when he was a scrivener?

   What symbolic meaning does this statement have?

 d. What does the narrator mean when he says that Bartleby has gone to sleep with "kings and counselors"?

 e. What does Bartleby's former job in the dead letter office symbolize?

5. a. Bartleby is clearly a man in need of help; without it, he dies. The narrator does not help Bartleby nearly as much as he should. How do his pride and self-absorption influence his refusal to help Bartleby fully?

 b. In the story, "Bartleby the Scrivener," Herman Melville is examining humanity. Just as pride keeps the narrator from assisting Bartleby, often this same trait keeps us from helping those less fortunate than ourselves. Write a few paragraphs telling about the human trait of pride and how it affects the world today.

1.

b. His attitude changes from one of self-satisfaction to shock and complete frustration.

c. Although there is a conflict between the narrator and Bartleby, the main conflict of the story is the internal conflict that is taking place within the narrator who is confused about how he should deal with Bartleby. The conflict would be classified as man vs. himself.

d. The writer builds the suspense through the conflicting emotions of the narrator. As Bartleby becomes less and less cooperative, the narrator constantly vacillates between dismissing him or not. When he finally dismisses him, and he does not leave, the narrator becomes increasingly frustrated with his inability to deal with the situation.

e. Answers will vary, but two examples follow:

The narrator is so consumed by the situation with Bartleby that he is caught up in the conversation of strangers on the street, assuming it is about the situation with Bartleby when in truth the conversation is completely unrelated.

The narrator is in such a state of nervous resentment that he feels he should check himself from further demonstrations.

f. Allow for discussion.

2.

b. Remembering the Scripture helps him from losing his temper with Bartleby. He realizes that because the Lord commands it, he has a responsibility to be kind to Bartleby even if he does not want to.

c. His friends begin to make comments about his decision to allow Bartleby to remain. The narrator becomes more concerned about how people perceive him rather than his responsibility to Bartleby.

d. He decides to move his offices elsewhere, thus ridding himself of Bartleby and leaving him to become someone else's problem.

e. He has no outward reaction. However, he refuses to leave the office even when new tenants move in.

f. "… something from within me upbraided me" (p. 126).
"I re-entered, with my hand in my pocket-and-and my heart in my mouth" (p. 127).
"I tore myself from him who I had so longed to be rid of" (p. 127).

3.

b. Bartleby stays, refusing to move. When he is put out of the office by the new tenant, he stays in the stairway during the day and sleeps in the entry at night. Eventually, he is moved to Tombs, a jail, under the charge of vagrancy.

c. He is concerned about how it would reflect on him if the story made the papers (p. 128).

d. Bartleby seems to be reaching out for continued contact with the narrator, begging him, in his quiet way, to continue speaking and offering help. The conversation, however, is cut short when the narrator loses patience and flies into a rage. Bartleby again closes his emotions and refuses to interact.

e. If you are staring at a wall, the view never changes. The wall symbolizes the wall of depression and "dead-end" feelings of Bartleby that keeps him from interacting with others. He does not know which way to turn for help, and his only security is found in the "dead-end" solution of no change.

4.

b. It is obvious to even Bartleby that the narrator knew he was in need of help and refused to give it. The narrator constantly viewed Bartleby's needs in context with his own self interests, and choosing, of course, to put his own interests first.

c. When Bartleby was a scrivener, he subsisted on a meager diet of ginger-nuts.

The author is using Bartleby's physical diet to symbolize his mental life. He is malnourished both physically and mentally and could not handle a full dinner of either food or conversation.

d. He is letting the reader know that Bartleby is dead and that he feels he has gone to heaven.

e. Bartleby was a man waiting in vain for a letter of kindness. The narrator, who was the "predestinated" sender of that letter, waited too long to send his letter (perhaps it was the truly selfless invitation to stay at his house). Like the dead letters, hope and help arrived too late, and Bartleby became a dead letter himself.

5.

a. In his pride, the narrator thinks only of his "masterly management" (p. 119) of the Bartleby situation. He is so painfully full of himself that he doesn't even think to help Bartleby as a human being. He assists him only as a business associate, offering him money instead of the compassion that he truly needs.

b. Answers will vary.

Teacher's Note: Please note that Mark Twain's writing contains the vernacular of his day, some of which might contain words that today's more enlightened society might find offensive. We suggest you preview the story and discuss this with your student.

1. a. Read "Baker's Bluejay Yarn" by Mark Twain (pp. 136-141).

   b. "Baker's Bluejay Yarn" combines both wit and humor. The narrator of the story was fashioned after a prospector, a master storysteller, with whom Mark Twain lived. Who is the narrator in this story? How does the author describe him?

   c. What talent did the narrator feel he possessed?

   d. According to the narrator, how does one identify a "good talker" among the animal kingdom?

   e. Which animal does the narrator identify as the best talker among the birds and animals?

   f. Define the following words from the story:

      1) gratification (p. 138)
      2) rudiments (p. 140)
      3) absurdity (p. 141)

2. a. Mark Twain, like James Thurber, the author of "The Catbird Seat," was a humorist. Compare and contrast the two stories. To **compare**, list the similarities of both stories. To **contrast** list the differences between the two.

   b. From what point of view is the story written?

   c. How does Mark Twain's use of dialect add to the story?

   d. Why does the narrator say that the bluejay is nearly as human as you or me? Give support for your answer.

   e. The author gives the bluejay a human personality. This literary device in which animals or objects are given human personality characteristics is called **personification**. Find two examples of personification in the story.
   Example: A jay will lie (p. 137).

f. Choose an animal and decide what sort of human personality characteristics you would give it. Write a few paragraphs describing the animal.

3. a. What is the conflict in "Baker's Bluejay Yarn"? How would it be classified?

   b. What other animal does the author compare with the jay?

      Compare and contrast the two animals.

   c. What does the jay do at the conclusion of the story that shows he has a sense of humor?

   d. What strong personality trait is evident in the jay who was trying to fill the hole? What is his weakest trait?

   e. What is your strongest personality trait? What is your weakest? Write a few paragraphs describing your personality. Support your description with reasons why you have chosen those personality traits, and give examples. Be sure to use descriptive language.

4. a. Mark Twain, a pseudonym for Samuel Clemens, led an interesting life. His experiences included growing up along the Mississippi River, working as a printer and a riverboat pilot. He also served in a local militia and was an unsuccessful prospector. The people he met, his experiences, and his vivid imagination gave him a wealth to draw from for his writing.

   b. How is "Baker's Bluejay Yarn" different from the other short stories you have read?

   c. Write a tall tale or any other story that would be considered an example of romanticism. For this story draw not only from personal experiences, but from your imagination. If you wish, you can use your description of an animal from **2f** and create a story around the animal's personality.

5. a. Continue working on your short story from **4c.** It is not necessary that you finish it today. You may take more time if necessary to complete the story.

    b. At one point in his life, Mark Twain did a series of humorous lectures on Hawaii. He would improve his lecture by changing his wording and timing to achieve the effect he wanted, often including dialect. He once said his method was "talking it and talking it and talking it till it sounds right."

    c. When you finish your story, read it aloud. Practice telling it aloud until you feel ready to present it to another person. Be sure to use dialect and expression in your voice to achieve your desired effect, then present the story to your teacher, family, or other group.

    d. Choose one of the vocabulary words to best replace the words in italics: gratification, rudiments, absurdity.

        1) The teacher felt immense *(pleasure)* _____ knowing her student had succeeded at the college.
        2) To build the house on the steep mountainside is a(n) *(foolish act)* _____.
        3) He had to understand the *(basic principles)* _____ of algebra before solving the problem.

. The narrator is Jim Baker. He is described by the author as being a middle-aged, simple-hearted miner who lives in an isolated wooded area of California (p. 136).

. He felt he could translate the conversations of the birds and animals (p. 136).

. A good talker is fluent and flowery, able to make comparisons and metaphors, has a large vocabulary, and shows off his talent by talking nonstop (p. 136).

. He feels the bluejay is the best talker because the bluejay is able to express his feelings in words, and he always uses good grammar (p. 137).

.

1) gratification - pleasure or satisfaction
2) rudiments - basic principles or skills
3) absurdity - a foolish or ridiculous action

2.

a. The two stories are alike in the way both stories have a humorous twist in the end.

They are different in that "The Catbird Seat" is about people and "Baker's Bluejay Yarn" is about animals.

b. The story is written in the first person point of view.

c. The use of dialect adds to the backwoods character of the narrator and gives the reader the feeling he is sitting on a pine stump in the middle of the woods of California listening to the miner tell his tale.

d. A bluejay has no principles.

Samples of support:
"A jay will lie, a jay will steal ..." (p. 137).
"A jay can cry, a jay can laugh, a jay can feel shame, a jay can reason and plan and discuss, a jay likes gossip and scandal, a jay has got a sense of humor, a jay knows when he is an ass just as well as you do—maybe better" (p. 138).

e. Answers may be any of the descriptions found on pp. 137-141.

f. Answers will vary.

3.
a. The jay found a hole in the roof of the house that he is determined to fill.

The conflict could be classified as man vs. nature since he is trying to fill a bottomless hole or man vs. man since it is his own stubbornness that causes the jay to continue an obviously hopeless task. The jay would be classified as "man" because he has been given a human personality by the author.

3.

b. The author compares the bluejay to a cat.

   The animals are similar in that they both normally use good grammar. However, the cat uses bad grammar whenever he is excited, while the jay seldom uses bad grammar, only in extreme circumstances.

c. When he is shown why he has been unable to fill the hole, instead of becoming frustrated and angry, "he fell over backwards suffocating with laughter" (p. 141).

d. The jay's strongest personality trait is his determination. No matter how difficult the task, he is determined to complete it.

   His weakest trait, however, is his stubbornness. Even when the hole would not fill, he continued in his fruitless task.

e. Answers will vary.

4.

b. As seen in the title, this is a tall tale or yarn. Unlike the other stories, which are examples of realism, this story is an example of romanticism. Romanticism is based more on an imaginary view of life, with heroes and happy endings. (See Lesson 4, 4d.) The story is completely fictional with the emphasis on imagination and emotions rather than on a real life situation.

c. Answers will vary.

d.
1) gratification
2) absurdity
3) rudiments

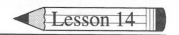

. a. Read "A Village Singer" by Mary Wilkins Freeman
   (pp. 191-207).

b. Mary Wilkins Freeman was a nineteenth century American
   novelist and author of short stories. She spent most of her
   young life in the small town of Randolph, Massachusetts, and
   her stories often reflect New England rural life during the late
   1800's.

. a. Look over pp. 191 to 196, ending with the paragraph
   beginning "Come along, Alma." Give a brief description of
   the following characters: Alma Way, William Emmons, Mr.
   Pollard, Wilson Ford, and Candace Whitcomb.

b. Would Candace Whitcomb be considered a flat or round
   character?

c. Does the author use the direct or indirect method to describe
   the characters in the story?

d. What is the conflict in "A Village Singer"?

e. Define the following words as used in the context of the story.

   1) perceptibly (p. 192)
   2) imperceptible (p. 194)
   3) pugnacious (p. 195)

   What root word is shared by the first two words? How does
   the addition of the suffix or prefix change each word?

. a. Look over pp. 196-201.

b. How does the author contrast how men and women are
   treated as they grow older?

c. How does Candace feel about the way in which the people of
   the church dismissed her?

d. How does the minister perceive Candace's outburst?

✐ **Teacher's Note:** The story refers to Wilson Ford and Alma as lovers. The term 'lovers' during the author's time was not used as in today's reference but rather as sweethearts.

4. a. Look over pp. 201-207.

   b. From what point of view is the story told? Give reasons for your choice.

   c. Freeman's stories often portray her Puritan religious background. Throughout the story the central character, Candace, accuses the church members as being responsible for the situation and the way she is being treated, but she never blames God. Find support throughout the story that supports this position.

   d. Often our actions speak louder than our words. The Word of God tells us to "... not love with word or with tongue, but in deed and truth" (I John 3:18). Write a few paragraphs telling the importance of showing kindness towards one another, particularly towards others within the family of God. Choose at least one Scripture passage to support what you are saying.

   e. Mary Freeman often included situations in her stories that dealt with the economic hardships of rural New England life. What situation in the story depicts this?

   f. What does the fire symbolize in this story?

   g. How did Candace's attitude change when she realized she was dying?

   h. List the different actions Candace takes in order to set things right before she dies.

   i. The character of Candace goes through many changes in this story. Write a few paragraphs describing the changes that take place.

a. To what is Candace compared in the last paragraph of the story? What was the author's meaning in this comparison?

b. Read the following first verse from the hymn, "Jesus, Lover of My Soul."

> *Jesus, lover of my soul,*
> *Let me to Thy bosom fly,*
> *While the nearer waters roll,*
> *While the tempest still is high,*
> *Hide me, O my Savior, hide,*
> *Till the storm of life is past;*
> *Safe into the haven guide,*
> *O receive my soul at last!*

Why do you think Candace chooses this hymn for Alma to sing to her?

c. Compare and contrast Alma with Candace by writing a list of ways they are similar and the ways they are different. After writing your lists, write two paragraphs.

d. Complete the following sentences using the correct vocabulary word: imperceptible, perceptibly, pugnacious.

1) The _____ children argued over which video to watch.
2) The deer's movement through the woods was

    _____.
3) The student was _____ quiet after receiving the final scores for the year.

2.

a.

1) Alma Way - the new leading soprano in the church. She is thin with blue eyes, blonde hair, and delicate features. She is no longer young as she is described as "beginning to look old" (p.195). Her personality is kind, shy, and meek.

2) William Emmons - the choir leader. He is described as being elderly, stout, and smooth-faced. As the "old musical dignitary of the village" (p 193), he is obviously stern and proud.

3) Mr. Pollard - the minister of the church. He is described as being a steady-faced, fleshy old man. His personality seems to be even-tempered but not forceful as he hesitantly states that "Miss Whitcomb—must be—reasoned with" (p.193).

4) Wilson Ford - the nephew of Candace Whitcomb and Alma Way's "lover" (p.194). He is described as being "a stout man with features so strong that they overcome his flesh." He has a rather arrogant, impatient personality as is evidenced by his attitude towards his aunt's behavior and the way he speaks to Alma.

5) Candace Whitcomb – a slender, elderly woman who has been the soprano in the church for forty years. She never married, but for many years William Emmons, the elderly choir leader, was her suitor. Although usually a quiet, submissive woman, her outburst to Mr. Pollard shows she is resolute and ambitious. She is not afraid to be straightforward in her assessment of the situation dealing with her replacement.

b. She would be considered a round character. Although the other characters in the story are unchanging, Candace is undergoing many changes in her personality.

c. The physical description is given in the indirect method and the personality is given in the direct method.

d. The conflict centers upon an older singer who has been replaced by a younger singer and refuses to gracefully accept losing her position.

e.
1) noticeably
2) unnoticeable
3) quarrelsome; belligerent

percept

The suffix -ible means *to be able* and the suffix -ly *means manner of.*

The prefix im- (in this particular word) means *not.*

3.

b. The pastor and Candace have both had their positions for forty years. In her discussion with the pastor, Candace mentions that he doesn't necessarily preach as well as he did forty years ago, but the congregation is not retiring him. She also brings out that the choir leader is also older, and yet he continues in his position.

She felt they were deceiving her by giving her the scrapbook and the party without letting her know why and then announcing in the letter that she was dismissed from her position. She would have preferred that they be honest and just tell her the truth outright.

He doesn't understand her feeling and is rather shocked by her outburst. He even feels that she is losing her senses.

It is told in third person omniscient.

The narrator tells you the thoughts of many of the different characters.

Answers will vary, but the following are examples of support.
On p. 198 Candace criticizes the congregation asking the minister what he thinks of "... folks that pretend to be Christians treatin' anybody the way they've treated me?".

On p. 201 Candace refuses to pray about the situation saying, "I don't think the Lord's got much to do with it anyhow."

Possible supporting Scriptures: Ephesians 4:2-3, I Corinthians 13:4-7, I John 4:7-8.

The situation with Candace's nephew, Wilson Ford, is an example of this hardship. He wants to marry Alma Way but cannot afford to marry her and take care of his mother, too (p. 203).

f. The fire is a symbol of time passing. The old is passing away as the new comes in.

g. Rather than hold onto her anger, she realizes that her life is ending, and she needs to seek forgiveness from those she has hurt.

h.
   1) She asks that the photo album be brushed up – showing a change in her attitude towards it and the people who gave it to her.
   2) She asks the minister to forgive her for the way she acted.
   3) She asks for Alma to come sing for her.
   4) She lets her nephew know that she is leaving the house to him when she dies and that Alma can have her things.

i. The character of Candace goes through many changes within the story. At first, singing is the most important thing in her life, and she jealously fights her replacement as soprano soloist in the church. She is resolute, straight forward, and ambitious, refusing to let go of her youth, position, and life itself. As the story progresses, and illness overtakes her, she changes her attitude toward her replacement and life. She becomes more passive and accepting. She acknowledges that her time has passed, and it is time for someone else to take her place. Her relationships are put in order, and finally, she accepts death willingly.

5.

a. She is compared to "... the old shape of a forest tree through the smoke and flame of the transfiguring fire the instant before it falls."

The author is showing the reader that like the tree in the fire, Candace's life was coming to an end. The foliage of youth has burned up, and it is time for life to come to an end.

b. Candace knows she is dying and is ready to meet the Lord. The hymn describes how she is feeling.

c. Paragraphs will vary but should contain some of the elements listed:

Similar – Both love music and have beautiful voices.
-They have never married, although both have had suitors.
- Both have been submissive and passive in their personalities.

Different – Although Alma enjoy music and singing, she does n have the passion for music tha Candace possesses (p. 202).
- Both women had suitors, but Candace's relationship was based mainly on she and her suitor loving music and singing together. Alma's relationship has more depth and is headed more towards marriage.
- Although both women behave in a submissive and passive manner, this was ruly Alma's personality while Candace "... held within herself the element of revolution" (p. 200). Candace was stubborn and had a fiery temper that was not evident before she was replaced.

d.
1) pugnacious
2) imperceptible
3) perceptibly

UNIT 2

The Novel

For The Novel Unit, you will need the following books:

The Red Badge of Courage, by Stephen Crane, published by Random House ISBN 9780553210118

The Old Man and the Sea, by Ernest Hemingway, published by Simon & Schuster ISBN 9780684801223

The Pearl, by John Steinbeck, published by Penguin Group ISBN 9780140177374

The Novel

Read the objectives for this section with your student. The same notebook can be used for this section as you used for The Short Story Unit. Continue to add vocabulary words and terms to the appropriate areas. The student will be analyzing the novels mostly through discussion, and therefore, there will be few writing assignments. Writing about one of the novels will be dealt with in the essay lessons.

Objectives

1) to help the student understand the difference between the short story and a novel
2) to examine the elements of a novel
3) to help the student identify and analyze the characters portrayed in a novel
4) to familiarize students with famous American novelists

Terms to Identify

novel
novella
stream of consciousness

The Red Badge of Courage by Stephen Crane
Published by Random House ISBN 9780553210118

Main Characters:

Henry Fleming - the hero of the story; a young man often referred to as the youth

Jim Conklin - (the tall soldier) a reassuring, fatherly figure to the youth; he was a friend of the youth since childhood; he is wounded in the second skirmish and dies later

The Tattered Soldier - a nameless, critically wounded man from another regiment; along with the youth, he witnesses the tall soldier's death

Wilson - (the loud soldier) an audacious, opinionated soldier before the battles; he is humbled and quieted after the first battle, and then honored for his bravery in a later battle

Stephen Crane wrote *The Red Badge of Courage*, his second novel, at the precocious age of twenty-one, astoundingly without ever having witnessed an actual battle. The novel is an utterly psychological account of a young private's passage into manhood. Crane delves deeply into the emotions and motivations of this youthful soldier, laying open for all eyes the horror, regret, and hope of war.

The novel opens with young Henry Fleming, green to the ways of war and having enlisted solely upon the strong wings of misguided passion and fervor, questioning his place in "one of those great affairs of the earth." He enlisted on a whim and is much heartened by the awe of his former schoolmates and the perceived sorrowful quiescence of a dark-haired girl. But now he doubts both his courage and place.

✐ Teacher Note: This section includes a summary of the complete novel. It will assist you in discussing the novel with the student. Also, some students are better able to understand the novel if they first read a summary, however, it should not replace reading the full novel. Please use this at your discretion.

The youth is moderately reassured by the tall soldier's affirmation that "... if a whole lot of boys started and run, why, I s'pose I'd start and run," but the youth still worries that he alone is suspicious of personal cowardice. Before the first battle, a particularly audacious soldier (Wilson) comes to the youth with a small packet. Much subdued after his first battle, the loud soldier humbly asks the youth to deliver the packet to his parents, for he is apparently divinely assured of death in the upcoming battle.

The youth survives the first battle physically and mentally and immediately deems himself worthy to partake in the long and glorious tradition of war. However, the particular rebel regiment quickly regroups and attacks again. This time, the youth runs. As he runs he assures himself that he has guessed right, that the regiment is doomed to utter annihilation. But he soon hears word that his regiment held their ground and were undefeated. Feeling that fate had betrayed him, he continues his journey, eventually surreptitiously joining another regiment in the woods which suffered losses. A tattered soldier walks beside him and, assuming he is out of place due to injury, kindly asks him where he was wounded. The youth shamefully escapes the tattered soldier and falls to the back of the procession. There, he finds his old friend, Jim Conklin, the tall soldier. Jim is wounded, and he soon madly dashes into the forest. Following him, the youth, now rejoined by the tattered soldier, witnesses the horrific death throes of his friend. Soon after, the tattered soldier begins to speak incoherently, and before the man falls victim to his wounds, the youth leaves him behind again.

He wanders aimlessly about, sullenly contemplating what derision will befall him if he rejoins his regiment. He encounters a fleeing host of men and is smashed on the head by one such fugitive when he stops him to question him. Dazed, he is accosted by a friendly, almost angelic figure whose face and name the youth never acquires. The angelic soldier brings the youth directly to his own camp where he finds the loud soldier and the rest of his regiment. Now that he has been injured, the youth no longer fears any mocking from the men, and he is pleased to let them assume his head was grazed by a musket ball.

He is grateful for the company of his friend, the loud soldier, but he finds that he has become much more temperate with experience. In the next skirmish that the regiment encounters, the youth asserts his bravery and high-standing among the men with a ferocious, unseeing assault upon the enemy. He is praised for his bravery, and in the next battle, both he and his friend save the colors from falling after the color sergeant is killed. Again, the youth, along with Wilson, is commended for his actions. Next, when the regiment charges the enemy, the youth again comes away with personal victory, stealing the colors from the enemy, as his own regiment again is victorious.

The men congratulate themselves, and Henry Fleming concludes that he has come of age. "He had been to touch the great death, and found that, after all, it was but the great death. He was a man." He no longer fears his old demons, and he denies his past philosophies. As the sun breaks free of the clouds, he feels he is reborn.

1. a. A **novel** is a fictional work of prose similar to a short story in form; however, a novel is more lengthy than a short story, usually containing a minimum of 50,000 words.

   b. Because a novel is usually longer than a short story, the author has more room to develop his story and his characters than in a short story. Plot development unfolds rather slowly, and the reader can gather information over larger units.

   c. This novel, *The Red Badge of Courage,* was written by Stephen Crane, the author of the short story, "The Open Boat." Since it is a short novel, it is sometimes called a **novella**. When beginning a novel, read carefully to pick up vital information.

   d. Read Chapter 1 of *The Red Badge of Courage.*

   e. Since this novel centers on the Civil War, we are tempted to think that the conflict is man vs. man. What is the real conflict in this story?

   f. How does the youth's (his real name is Henry Fleming) attitude change from the beginning of the chapter to the end?

   g. Define the following vocabulary words as used in the context of the story.

   1) doggedly (p. 5)
   2) effaced (p. 6)

2. a. Read Chapters 2 and 3 of the novel.

   b. In Chapter 2, Henry has great anxiety over his fear of battle. How does he try to deal with this fear, beginning on page 12?

   c. When the men begin maneuvers for battle, what happens to Henry's sense of participation in the preparation?

   d. Define the following vocabulary words as used in the context of the story.

   1) flouted (p. 12)
   2) vociferous (p. 15)
   3) perambulating (p. 20)
   4) declamation (p. 23)

3. a. Read Chapters 4-5.

   b. Chapter 4 shows us that the enemy forces are quite large. How do we know this?

   c. Chapter 5 provides a highly realistic glimpse of a skirmish and the emotions, sounds, and sights that normally occur. This chapter should be read just to admire Crane's ability to recreate a battle scene using only words. Note that Henry has changed from feeling alienated to feeling as if he is part of a unit (page 32).

      What is the point of the last paragraph in Chapter 5?

   d. Define the following vocabulary words as used in the context of the story.

      1) banshee (p. 28)
      2) facetious (p. 29)
      3) respite (p. 33)
      4) débris (p. 35)

4. a. Read Chapters 6-7.

   b. On pages 43, 44, and 45, Henry is angry because he was wronged and rationalizes his actions. What emotion is Henry really dealing with?

   c. Why is the encounter with the dead soldier significant at this point in the story?

   d. Define the following vocabulary words as used in the context of the story.

      1) affably (p. 37)
      2) sagacious (p. 44)

5. a. Read Chapters 8-9.

   b. How is Henry's absorption into the wounded ranks actually a
      blessing rather than a curse?

   c. How does Henry's discovery of the dead soldier in Chapter 7
      foreshadow Jim Conklin's death?

   d. Define the following vocabulary words as used in the
      context of the story.

      1) doggerel (p. 49)
      2) sardonic (p. 50)
      3) spectral (p. 53)
      4) ague (p. 56)

6. a. Read Chapters 10-11.

   b. In Chapter 10, why is the tattered man's condition so pitiful?

   c. Why is Henry particularly sensitive about questions regarding
      his wounds at this point?

   d. In Chapter 11, Henry considers many scenarios for
      recovering his self-confidence. What do you think he should
      do?

   e. Define the following vocabulary words as used in the
      context of the story.

      1) harangue (p. 59)
      2) malediction (p. 62)

7. a. Read Chapters 12-13.

   By this time, it is obvious that Henry has been given a second chance. He was fortunate and became an honored hero and a symbol of hope to his regiment. Crane made us feel a strong sense of desire to see Henry make a comeback from his retreat. Perhaps we feel this largely because Henry went through an experience that could very well have been our own, and we feel a strong identity with him. At any rate, Henry's internal conflict is greatly increased, because all of his weaknesses are exposed. Perhaps he only learned how to survive without paying a price for it. Perhaps he learned something about himself that he will correct. At this point we don't know because Henry is truly a round, complex character whose actions cannot be predicted like a flat character. Henry is capable of self-analysis and redirection.

   Let's see what he does with his recent experience behind him.

   b. Read Chapters 14-15.

   c. Why do you think Crane shows Henry in parallel scenes with Wilson (the loud soldier)?

   d. Define the following vocabulary words as used in the context of the story.

   1) lurid (p. 68)
   2) crone (p. 77)
   3) peremptory (p. 79)
   4) lugubrious (p. 83)

8. a. Read Chapters 16-17.

   b. Although Henry's denunciation of a general whom he doesn't know seems foolish, it is actually a good sign. What does this behavior indicate?

   c. Henry regards himself as having attained hero status by the end of Chapter 17. What do you think? Support your answer with evidence from the text.

d. Define the following vocabulary words as used in the context of the story.

   1) fracas (p. 87)
   2) trundled (p. 90)
   3) repose (p. 92)
   4) abominable (p. 93)

9. a. Read Chapters 18-20.

   b. The conversation between the general and his officer on pp. 98 and 99 reveals that Henry's company has received an extremely dangerous assignment. Give at least four reasons why we know this.

   c. How do we know that Henry has really changed by the end of Chapter 19?

   d. In Chapter 20, Henry must stop fighting in order to carry the battle flag. Why is it such an act of bravery to carry it?

   e. What do you think Crane means by the last sentence in Chapter 20?

   f. Define the following vocabulary words as used in the context of the story.

   1) dexterous (p. 98)
   2) gesticulating (p. 100)
   3) accouterments (p. 101)
   4) imprecations (p. 104)
   5) mêlée (p. 107)

10. a. Read Chapter 21 to the end of the book.

   Chapter 21 is a good illustration of how our identity can be influenced by what others think of us. When Henry heard the taunts of the other soldiers, he suddenly felt that the ground his company had gained was "trivial and ridiculous." When he heard what his commanders think of him, however, notice how his self-esteem returns.

b. What ominous meaning can we derive from Henry's fantasy on page 121?

c. Find at least two places in Chapter 22 which reinforce Henry's imagined calculation that he will likely be killed.

d. What symbolic event shows us that the battle is over?

e. Do you recall how Henry was wounded and what he said about it in Chapters 12 and 13? Do you think Henry has earned the right to claim that he has a "red badge of courage"?

f. Define the following vocabulary words as used in the context of the story.

   1) bated (breath) (p. 114)
   2) celerity (p. 120)
   3) stoical (p. 126)
   4) clover (p. 130)

1.

e. The real conflict is the youth's internal conflict regarding his fitness as a solider.
   man vs. himself

f. His attitude changes from the idealistic thoughts of the glory of war to extreme fear of the reality of battle.

g.
   1) doggedly - stubbornly
   2) effaced - erased

2.

b. He deals with his fear by trying to find others who are similarly fearful.

c. Henry feels "separated" (p. 15), "pity for himself" (p. 16), and "a mental outcast" (p. 18).

d.
   1) flouted – scorned
   2) vociferous – shouting noisily; clamorous
   3) perambulating – walking around inspecting
   4) declamation – a formal speech

3.

b. The enemy forced everyone to retreat.

c. Nature is indifferent to the struggles of man. This is a point made often in "The Open Boat."

d.
   1) banshee – a female spirit believed to wail and warn of an impending death
   2) facetious – lightly joking in an inappropriate time
   3) respite – relief
   4) débris – scattered remains

4.

b. Fear. Henry deeply regrets that he gave into cowardice too soon. If he had stayed he probably would have made it.

c. Answers may vary, but the following may be helpful. Henry is running from the war, and the soldier reminds him that he can't escape. Furthermore, Henry is reminded that he hasn't done his part, whereas the dead soldier has given everything. Henry knows that he could have been killed in combat, but because he ran, someone else might have died in his place. Perhaps Henry feels that he should have died, knowing that the others needed him.

d.
   1) affably – pleasantly
   2) sagacious – shrewd

5.

b. Henry is angry with himself for turning coward. This is a way for him to re-enter the fighting ranks without being detected for desertion.

c. The soldier Henry discovered in Chapter 7 obviously had died slowly. He had time to go off by himself and choose his last resting place, as Jim did. Both chose little places where the foliage was inviting. Furthermore, both had the same look in their eyes as if seeing into the beyond.

1) doggerel – a trivial verse or
   jingle usually comic in nature
2) sardonic – disdainfully
   sarcastic
3) spectral – ghostly
4) ague – fit of shivering

He is dying slowly and leaving
behind a wife and family whom
he obviously loves and for
whom he feels a great
responsibility. Also, even Henry
rejects him in the end, leaving
him to die alone and unattended.

Jim and the tattered soldier have
not only been wounded, but
mortally wounded. They have
given everything in the line of
duty, and Henry must endure his
own cowardice in the face of
these genuine heroes.

Answers may vary greatly, but
the following is a possible
answer: There is nothing Henry
can do; however, Henry needs to
go back to the fighting and put
his fear and self-pity behind him.

1) harangue – a long pompous
   speech
2) malediction – curse

The actual fighting changed both
of them. Both became greatly
humbled by their respective
experiences, but this has a
positive effect. Both became
less conscious of themselves
and more conscious of others.
Henry's willingness to give back
Wilson's letters without pressing
the advantage is the best
illustration of this change in him.

d.
   1) lurid – violent
   2) crone – withered old woman
   3) peremptory – commanding
   4) lugubrious – mournful

8.
b. Henry is eager to fight and to
   win. Although his harangue is
   nonsense, he wants every
   advantage when the fighting
   begins.

c. Answers may vary greatly, but
   the following is a possible
   answer.
   Henry has shown great courage
   and determination, but he has
   not been tested severely enough
   to grant hero status at this point.

d.
   1) fracas – brawl
   2) trundled – rolled
   3) repose – rest
   4) abominable - loathsome

9.
b.
   1) They are being used to fortify
      a spot where the enemy is
      strong enough to break
      through.
   2) It will be "hell to pay"
      stopping them.
   3) Henry's fellow soldiers fight
      like "mule drivers." They're
      poor soldiers.
   4) The company is being ordered
      to charge.
   5) The general doesn't believe
      "many of your mule drivers
      will get back."

9.

c. We discovered in Chapter 18 that Henry's company is in grave danger. Don't overlook the fact that Henry overheard the conversation, and he also knows of the extreme danger. Nevertheless, Henry fixes his gaze where he thinks the enemy is, and charges, actually leading the company. This is not the same person who turned and ran in panic in Chapter 6.

d. Since Henry can't carry a weapon and a flag at the same time, he can't defend himself. Furthermore, a good flag carrier stays in the front ranks of battle, and has a greater risk of being shot. Moreover, the flag is easily seen by the enemy.

e. He does not mean that they are insignificant and lowly — mere men in the midst of something much greater than themselves. Rather, he means that they have reached maturity. They have been tested and have passed from novices to veteran soldiers.

f.
1) dexterous – having skill in using the hand or body
2) gesticulating – using gestures to help express one's meaning
3) accouterments – all of a soldier's equipment except clothes and weapons
4) imprecations – cursings
5) mêleé - a confused hand-to-hand fight

10.

b. There is a high probability that Henry will die on the battlefield

c. At the bottom of page 120, Cran tells us that the enemy began to "slice up the blue men."
On page 121, we are told that "Grunting bundles of blue bega to drop."
On page 121, some men "… fell down about the feet of their companions."
Also, illustrations such as the wounded sergeant and other less specific passages can be used to suggest the intensity o the battle.

d. It is shown when Wilson captures the other company's flag. The position and possession of the company flag has been a major point since Henry began bearing his own company's flag. Now the enemy's flag is also in his (his friend's) possession.

e. Answers will vary.

f.
1) bated (breath) – breath held i because of fear or excitemen
2) celerity – quickness
3) stoical – showing indifferenc to joy, pain, etc.
4) clover – living a carefree life

The Old Man and the Sea by Ernest Hemingway
Published by Simon and Schuster ISBN 9780684801223

Main Characters:

Santiago - the old man, a fisherman
Manolin - a young boy, the old man's dear and only friend

He is an old man who fishes alone in a skiff in the Gulf Stream
and he has gone eighty-four days now without taking a fish. Thus
begins Hemingway's tremendous tale of an old fisherman and the
epic struggle between man and nature, nature taking the form of an
enormous marlin. Probably Hemingway's most well known work,
this novel is written in Hemingway's customarily simplistic and,
simultaneously, forceful style.

Set in and around the island of Cuba, only two characters have more
than two lines: the boy, Manolin, and the old man, occasionally
referred to by the boy by his Christian name, Santiago, but, for the
most part, referred to simply as "old man." The old man endured
twelve full weeks without landing a fish, enduring also the ridicule
of the younger fishermen on the island. The boy's parents have
forced young Manolin to work on another boat, determining the old
man to be incurably unlucky. The boy, however, remains a faithful
and loving friend to the old man. Acquiescent with Hemingway's
stark styling, their conversations are seemingly conducted with
utmost gravity, yet tenderness and satisfaction are evident to the
attentive reader. The old man and the boy discuss their two favorite
topics, fishing and baseball.

As the story opens, the two friends discuss baseball and the "lucky"
eighty-fifth day which, the old man hopes, will bring an end to his
ill-fortune. He goes to bed early and dreams. The old man once
dreamed of women and storms and great fish and arm wrestling and
of his wife and other great things that departed many years ago.
Now that he is old, he dreams only of two things: nearby islands
and harbors and lions playing on the beach. Even though he loves
the dream lions as much as he loves the boy, he never dreams about
the boy.

✐ **Teacher Note: This
section includes a summary
of the complete novel. It will
assist you in discussing the
novel with the student. Also,
some students are better
able to understand the novel
if they first read a summary,
however, it should not
replace reading the full
novel. Please use this at
your discretion.**

Under cover of early morning darkness, he is full of hope as he embarks on the greatest fishing expedition of his life. The old man has a great respect for nature; he feels sympathy for the sea birds, believing them too fragile to survive the cruel enormity of the ocean. Yet at the same time, he recognizes the ocean as the majestic, generous patron of fishermen. He refers to the ocean in the feminine, la mar, which is what people call her in Spanish when they love her. He baits four lines at descending depths, and by late morning, the old man has far out-distanced all the other fishing boats. He plans to fish amongst schools of small albacore and bonito, hoping that the great fish, the noble marlin which is his due, will be with them.

When the green shore has fully disappeared behind the blue hills of the ocean, the old man hooks into the great fish. From this point until nearly the end of the story, the old man wages a physically tortuous battle against the great fish and then an equally painful emotional battle against predacious sharks. For days, the old man fights the fish, always admiring the nobility of the fearsome creature, always intent on killing it. The old man fights through maddening weariness, numbing cramps, near-starvation and dehydration and numerous other pains and sores as he fights the fish. He pleads with the fish and blesses it; he prays to the Virgin Mary for the fish's death, and, when it dies, he laments the creature's passing.

Soon after he lands the fish, the sharks arrive. Although the old man kills many of them, they tear into the once beautiful fish and devour nearly all the meat, leaving behind a skeleton eighteen feet long. With abject sorrow, the old man apologizes to the fish, acknowledging that, in his excitement and haste, he went too far into the ocean. His body has been strained nearly beyond its limit, and as he kills the last shark, he curses the ocean, saying, ".... make a dream you've killed a man." With no weight to slow him, he sails quickly. After making landfall, he trudges up the hill to his home, carrying his mast upon his wounded shoulders, like a cross upon the shoulders of another man, long ago.

e sleeps through the night and into the next morning, when the
oy finds him. The other fishermen see the giant carcass and
raise Santiago. But the boy, crying shamelessly over his friend's
ain, only walks back to bring coffee to the old man. When the
ld man awakes, he tells the boy that the sharks beat him, but the
sh did not. He gives the spear to the boy. Later that day, a
oman spots the great skeleton in the water, with its majestic tail
aving slowly with the tide. When told it was a shark, she
xclaims that she never knew sharks had such beautiful tails.
Meanwhile, the old man is sleeping, dreaming of lions playing on
he beach.

. Find a reference book and read about the life of Ernest
Hemingway. It is always helpful to read some background
information about the author. Some reference books might
give information about an author's major themes and topics,
providing keys to understanding the works. (In the Simon &
Schuster publication, you will find a page titled "About the
Author" on the last page of the book.)

. a. Read pp. 9-18 of *The Old Man and the Sea*. Stop in the
middle of page 18 where the boy tells the old man he will go
for the sardines.

b. What is the conflict in this story?

c. Why does the boy love the old man?

d. What is the significance of the boy's recollection of his first
fishing trip?

e. What kind of fish does Santiago fish for?

f. What are some characteristics of the old man that show us he
is a good fisherman?

. a. Read from page 18 to the top of page 28.

b. The boy cares for Santiago by bringing food from the Terrace
Restaurant. How do we know that this is a popular and
prosperous restaurant?

c. How has Hemingway used the method of foreshadowing t give clues to the reader that Santiago is due for a great catch

d. How old do you think the boy is now?

e. What do you learn of Santiago by observing his dreams?

4. a. Read from page 28; stop at the top of page 41.

   b. What is the setting of this story?

   c. What is the significance of the setting in terms of the confli

   d. How does Hemingway express Santiago's intimacy with th sea?

   e. What signs indicate changes for Santiago?

   f. In the short story, "The Open Boat," by Stephen Crane, we considered the concept of fate as a directive force. Here another word is used which might be a synonym for fate. What is it?

   g. Do you think Hemingway and Crane are similar in their spiritual understanding?

   h. Consider your viewpoint on fate. How does this apply to *The Old Man and the Sea*?

5. a. Read from page 41 to the bottom of page 52.

   b. Santiago's intimate knowledge of fishing and his great strength of character are demonstrated in this segment of th novel. However, there is another character that must be examined. Describe the fish in as many ways as you can, including its abstract characteristics, such as intelligence, etc

   c. Santiago's recollection of the male marlin that followed its mate to the end suggests things about the fish he has presently caught. What are they?

d. What do you make of Santiago's statement that he will stay with the fish until he (Santiago) is dead?

a. Read from page 53 to the top of page 66.

b. In several places, Santiago expresses his great admiration and love for the fish, but he knows he must kill it. Why does Santiago love the fish?

c. Why does the fish jump?

d. Notice Santiago's communion with and understanding of nature. We are presented with the portrait of a man who identifies with nature as one who knows his place in nature, yet keeps his identity as a human who is separated from nature by his intellect and social accomplishments.

a. Read from page 66 to the top of page 80.

b. This segment of the story is a good example of **stream-of-consciousness**. This is the technique of developing the character's thoughts as they occur, much as people do in normal thought patterns. This flow of thought may move from fragments to complete sentences. Modern writers are fond of this technique, which gives writing a realistic aspect.

c. The arm-wrestling match on pp. 69 to 70 foreshadows the match with the fish. How does Hemingway hint to show us that the arm-wrestling match is a foreshadow?

a. Read from page 80 to the top of page 110.

b. Did Santiago accomplish anything by bringing in the marlin and killing it? Support your answer with evidence from the story.

c. Compare and contrast the marlin and the Mako shark.

d. Do you think Santiago will get any portion of the marlin to market?

9. a. Read the rest of the story.

   b. Do you think Santiago's misfortune will turn out for the best after all?

   c. Do you think Santiago is a hero?

   d. If you are able, view the movie version of *The Old Man and the Sea* starring Spencer Tracy.

✐**Teacher's Note:**
We advise you to preview the movie to decide if it is appropriate for your student.

10. a. If you were able to view the movie, compare the movie to the book. Do you feel that the movie was an adequate representation of the book? In what ways did the movie enhance your understanding of the story?

    b. If you were unable to view the movie, write a brief book review. Use the following questions as a guide to writing a good review.

       1) What is the title of the novel?
       2) Who is the author?
       3) What was the setting?
       4) Who were the main characters?
       5) What was the plot?
       6) What was the author trying to say in the story?
       7) What is your opinion of the book? Support your opinion with examples or quotes from the book.

. The old man, Santiago, makes his living by fishing. He went eighty-four days without catching a fish. Already poor, the dry stretch is very hard for him and he must depend on others for food, bait, etc. We can categorize this as man vs. nature.

c. Santiago taught the boy how to fish when he was very young, and the relationship developed from there.

d. He recalls it in detail because it made a great impression on him and is a point of intimacy between him and Santiago. It is a sign of his love for the old man. The "fiction" and the baseball are similar points of intimacy he and Santiago share.

e. Marlin are first on the list, but apparently sharks or dolphins will do. The point is that he goes after big fish that cannot be taken in by the gross, such as snapper; therefore are less dependable as a constant source of income.

f. He has vast experience and "knows many tricks." He is patient and determined, going out day after day without giving up.

3.
b. Because some of the greatest baseball players of all time like to visit there.

c. We are told repeatedly that 85 is a lucky number. Furthermore, September is the month when the "great fish come," and we are reminded that Santiago's age is taking his strength, but he "knows many tricks" that will enable him to land a big fish.

d. He is about 16 to 18 years old. He is old enough to play Big League baseball, but not old enough to leave his parents.

e. He apparently has had an adventurous life and a good marriage. These memories are so far in the past that he no longer dreams of them. His life has taken on a simplicity that he is content with.

4.
b. The setting is a small skiff off the shore of Havana, Cuba.

c. Santiago is alone and very vulnerable. Although he is highly skilled and experienced, he depends on good fortune for survival.

d. Santiago held great knowledge and admiration for the sea. He always referred to the sea as "la mar." He regarded her as a woman that gives or withholds favors.

e. The bird, the school of dolphin, the plankton, and the school of tuna all signify great activity surrounding Santiago. Even the weather is in his favor. He's already caught a small tuna. Maybe this is his day.

4.

f. luck

g. Allow for discussion.

h. Allow for discussion.

5.

b. The fish is great in size and strength. He has great endurance, patience, and resolve. Moreover, Santiago attributes wisdom to the fish because the fish won't tire itself by jumping nor will it act foolishly by panicking. Santiago also feels that the fish has chosen a destination that will help it to win the fight.

(It is acceptable to attribute characterictics to the fish such as kindness, sympathy, faithfulness, etc.)

c. Santiago thinks the fish he has caught is also a male. Therefore, he might be equally as devoted to a cause and determined to stay with it until all hope is lost. Also, there is an intelligence and sensitivity shown by this that goes beyond what we normally expect of a fish.

d. Although Santiago possesses great resolve to finish what he has started, the outcome of the struggle is in doubt. There is a question as to who will win, and if Santiago will make it back even if he does land the fish.

6.

b. Santiago admires the great creature. Also, Santiago knows the dollar value that the marlin will bring. Most significantly, Santiago identifies with the fish.

Both he and the fish endure grea hardship and suffering, struggling for their very lives against great odds.

c. This is a loaded question. Sometimes we forget that fiction is artificial. Hemingway has Santiago answer this question: to show how big the fish is. Hemingway wants the reader to see the fish, making it more vivi and lifelike.

7.

c. First, it is a great endurance contest, going far beyond what most people can tolerate. The size and strength of Santiago's opponent compare to the marlin. The negro's move which Santiago recovered from can be compared to the jump of the marlin. Most importantly, notice that Santiago is preparing himself for the fish to "make his effort (bottom of page 75), and that the fish is "tiring" or "resting" (page 79), so that it is not long before the marlin makes a final thrust.

8.

b. Answers will vary, but the following may be helpful. Most people feel that Hemingway wants you to admire Santiago's costly victory. However, you might think differently. Remember, Santiago could have given up at any time. Had he cut the marlin loose and hauled in the second fish that he hooked, he might be home now, with money in his pocket.

Similarities involve their great size, strength, determination, beauty, etc.

The difference is the marlin represents good, but the shark represents evil.

Answers will vary.

Even Santiago has given up hope of this, yet he persists in trying with all his might. This is a prevalent Hemingway theme — persisting in a course of action even though the obstacles are enormous. Once Santiago decides to land the fish, it becomes the right thing for him to do. He admits he went out too far, but he persists in seeing his mission to completion.

9.
b. **Answers will vary.**

c. **Answers will vary.**

10.
a. **Allow for discussion**

b. **Answers will vary.**

The Pearl by John Steinbeck
Published by the Penguin Group
ISBN 9780140177374

Main Characters:

Kino - a poor Indian pearl diver
Juana - Kino's wife
Coyotito - Kino and Juana's baby
Juan Tomás - Kino's older brother
Apolonia - Juan Tomás' wife
The doctor - the local doctor; greedy; from a different race than Kino

✐ **Teacher Note: This section includes a summary of the complete novel. It will assist you in discussing the novel with the student. Also, some students are better able to understand the novel if they first read a summary, however, it should not replace reading the full novel. Please use this at your discretion.**

Kino is a poor Indian living in the outskirts of a seaside town in Mexico. His wife, Juana, and their baby, Coyotito, share his brush house. Making a meager living as a pearl diver, his life is probably much the same as it has been for generations. Society conveniently dictated that poverty would greet him and his children's children. Life is simple, one day not very different from the next, but there is peace.

When Coyotito is stung by a scorpion, Kino and Juana boldly walk to town to see the doctor. They are refused because they have no money. Their problems appear to be resolved when Kino finds a pearl of great worth. But in reality, this begins the end of the simple, yet peaceful existence they have known. The pearl brings suspicion, hatred, anger, greed, and murder. Although Juana and his brother, Juan Tomás, plead with Kino to destroy the pearl, Kino persists that this will end his miseries. The pearl, which at first seemed like a gift from the gods, ends up destroying them and everything they held truly valuable.

1. a. Read Chapter 1.

   b. If you are not familiar with the following words, look them up in the dictionary.

      1) covey (p. 1)
      2) pulque (p. 4)
      3) plaintively (p. 5)
      4) bougainvillaea (p. 8)
      5) suppliant (p. 12)

   c. Review page 1 to the last paragraph on page 4, and describe Kino's life. Describe the likely events of a day, his conversations, and his feelings.

   d. When Juana saw the scorpion, she spoke an ancient magic and a Hail Mary. What does this mean to you in regards to her beliefs?

   e. What is the significance of the "Song of the Family" and the "Song of Evil"?

   f. What was Juana's reaction to the scorpion sting and why did it cause such a commotion?

   g. Describe Kino's thoughts as he knocked on the doctor's door.

   h. Why do you think the doctor's servant refused to speak to Kino in his native tongue, but spoke in it later?

2. a. Contrast the doctor's home with Kino's home. Steinbeck provided some descriptions and details. Use this to write two descriptive paragraphs.

   b. When the servant returned to the doctor with the folded paper of pearls, he quickly returned to Kino. Write a paragraph describing what may have taken place. Include dialogue if you wish.

3. a. Read Chapter 2.

   b. If you are unfamiliar with the following words, look them u[p] in the dictionary.

      1) estuary (p. 13)
      2) lateen (p. 13)
      3) bulwark (p. 14)
      4) undulating (p. 17)
      5) hummock (p. 18)

   c. Why is Kino's canoe so valuable to him?

   d. What was the significance of "The Song of the Pearl that Might Be"?

   e. Before Kino opened the great oyster, Juana looked away because she thought it not good to want a thing too much. What does this tell you about their concept of the gods?

   f. Describe the thoughts that may have played in Kino's mind [as] he was opening the oyster.

4. a. Steinbeck repeatedly mentions illusion versus reality. Wha[t] does this mean to you?

   b. Describe the dreams you think Kino saw on the surface of t[he] great pearl.

5. a. If you are unfamiliar with the following words, look them u[p] in the dictionary.

      1) disparagement (p. 25)
      2) subjugation (p. 30)
      3) dissembling (p. 32)

   b. Read Chapter 3.

   c. Why did the pearl make Kino every man's enemy?

   d. The pearl brings evil into the town. How is this evil like the scorpion?

e. How was it like "hunger in the smell of food"?

f. How was it like "loneliness when love is withheld"?

g. What pictures does Kino see in the pearl?

6. a. After Kino's visions in the pearl, Steinbeck says that Kino is afraid as a man is afraid who says, "I will," without knowing. What does this mean to you?

    Consider Proverbs 19:21, "Many are the plans in a man's heart, but the counsel of the Lord, it will stand."

   b. When the doctor arrives at Kino's hut, Kino is enraged and refuses to let him in. Why does he change his mind?

   c. Compare Juana's reaction to the pearl in the beginning of the story to her reaction at the end of this chapter.

7. a. Read Chapter 4.

   b. If you are unfamiliar with the following words, look them up in the dictionary.

       1) legerdemain (p. 48)
       2) collusion (p. 50)

   c. How did Kino feel when the appraiser offered him a thousand pesos for the pearl?

   d. Do you think Kino should have taken the final offer of fifteen hundred pesos? Explain.

   e. Why was Kino afraid of the capital?

   f. How did Juan Tomás feel about Kino's refusal of the appraiser's offer and his decision to go to the capital?

8. a. It is pertinent to understand the social economic climate of Kino's world. It is easy for us to agree with Kino's decision to seek justice. But fifteen hundred pesos would be a considerable amount of money for him, and it would be a sure thing. Do you think he did the right thing? Explain.

   b. Kino repeatedly says, "I am a man." What do you think he means?

9. a. If you are unfamiliar with the following word, look it up in the dictionary.

   edifice (p. 63)

   b. Read Chapter 5.

   c. After the struggle on the beach, Juana knows that the old life is gone forever. Why?

   d. Why was Kino so enraged when he saw that his canoe had been destroyed?

   e. What do you think Kino meant at the end of the chapter when he said, "This pearl has become my soul..."?

10. a. Read Chapter 6.

    b. Kino looked in his pearl to see his vision again. Compare and contrast what he wanted to see with what he actually did see.

1) covey - a small flock of birds
2) pulque - a fermented drink made from the juice of a desert plant
3) plaintively - sorrowfully
4) bougainvillaea - (also spelled bougainvillea) a tropical vine with colorful, showy flowers
5) suppliant - submissive

Kino's life is simple. One day is probably very much the same as another. Kino and his family live in poverty, his meals are simple, words are few, but there is peace.

She is deeply rooted in the superstitious beliefs of her ancestors, yet attains the newer ways of thinking probably brought on by Catholic missions.

The "Song of the Family" assumes their life together in simplicity and tradition.
The "Song of Evil" is the music of the enemy, that which would come against family, friends, and goodness.

Juana immediately took care of the baby and then told Kino to get the doctor. To request a doctor caused a stir because poor folks like themselves did not do things that were reserved only for the rich. This was a brave and noble request.

g. Kino acknowledges his own Indian background and realizes all that it symbolizes. He knows too, that the doctor is of the race who put Kino and his people in "their place." He feels fear and anger.

h. Perhaps the servant was trained not to use his native tongue to assume a civilized appearance. Or perhaps the servant chose to deny his native tongue to maintain his dignity as the doctor's servant. You may have other thoughts.

Perhaps later the servant felt shame about not speaking, or maybe he used it out of consideration to ease the news for Kino.

2.
a. Answers will vary.

b. Answers will vary.

3.
b.

1) estuary - the wide lower part of a river into which the tide flows
2) lateen - a triangular sail
3) bulwark - something that serves as a principal defense
4) undulating - rising and falling in a wavelike manner
5) hummock - a low, rounded hill

c. With a canoe, he is able to provide food for his family. Also, the canoe belonged to his father and grandfather.

d. It was a song of hope. Although the chance was slight, the gods might allow it.

e. Answers will vary. Perhaps she feels unworthy to receive something good from the gods. Perhaps she didn't want to appear greedy.

f. Answers will vary.

4.

a. Answers will vary. Encourage your student to think deeply on this one.

b. Kino saw hope. He saw a new life for himself and his family. The pearl was the answer to his meager existence.

5.

a.
   1) disparagement - belittlement
   2) subjugation - enslavement
   3) dissembling - hiding the truth

c. The pearl now separates Kino from every man. Kino owns the great pearl; the others have none. The pearl brings lust, envy, and greed.

d. It brought death.

e. It brought greed.

f. It brought pain.

g. He sees a marriage in a church. He sees a harpoon and a rifle. He sees his son going to school. He sees his son reading to his parents.

6.

a. Answers will vary.

b. The doctor is able to convince Kino that he is ignorant and the doctor has the knowledge and means to cure Coyotito. As Steinbeck says, "The trap was set."

c. At first, Juana is happy and excited. But slowly she sees how it is changing their lives and the evil it has brought.

7.

b.
   1) legerdemain - sleight of hand; trickery
   2) collusion - secret agreement for fraudulent purposes

c. He was angry and suspicious. "He felt the creeping of fate, the circling of wolves, the hover of vultures."

d. Answers will vary.

e. Kino knows he is only a poor, uneducated Indian. His life up to this point has been simple and small. He has never been far from home.

f. Juan Tomás feels uneasy about Kino's decision. He realizes that Kino will be embarking in unknown territory, stepping out from the small world he knows.

8.

a. Allow for discussion.

b. He is willing to fight for what he feels is rightfully his.

edifice - any large, imposing
construction

. Juana recognizes what the pearl
has brought into their lives: anger,
hatred, suspicions, and most of all,
murder. Their lives could never be
the same.

. It was his one possession of worth.
Originally his grandfather's, the
canoe had been plastered over and
over. If a canoe is destroyed, it is
of no use.

. Allow for discussion.

0.
. He wanted to see a rifle, but he saw
the body of the man he killed.
Instead of seeing a church
marriage, he saw Juana's face,
bruised by his own hand. He
wanted to see Coyotito reading,
but he saw his son feverish from
the doctor's "medicine."

UNIT 3

The Essay

The Essay Unit is divided into three parts:

1. The Expository Essay - Lessons 21-22
2. The Descriptive Essay - Lessons 29-30
3. The Narrative Essay - Lessons 34-35

The Essay

Read the objectives with your student. Make sure he understands that he will be writing three different kinds of essays with the first one being an expository essay. The other two essays will be written in Lessons 29-30 and Lessons 34-35. The notebook will be used for the student to add unfamiliar terms in section three. Also, the essays are written in the fourth section. Two lessons are designated for each essay. Although the same number format that appears in previous lessons is used, the lessons are not divided according to days. Work through the material at a speed that is appropriate for the student. Once the student has completed his essay, use the assessment provided at the end of each essay section to help in evaluating the student's work.

Note

The essay is a method of logical thought presentation using various rhetorical techniques such as comparison and contrast, extended definition, argument and persuasion, etc. By now, you are probably familiar with correct grammar and sentence structure; therefore, let's focus on organizing thoughts in a clear, understandable progression.

Objectives

1) to guide the student in a logical thought process
2) to teach the student various rhetorical techniques
3) to show by example an outline of a topic
4) to encourage the student in editing this paper

Terms to Identify

expository essay
introductory paragraph
body paragraph
concluding paragraph
topic sentence
subtopics
concluding sentence
topic
introduction
supportive topics
conclusion
transitional words
thesis statement
rough draft
final draft
descriptive essay
narrative essay

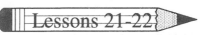
The Expository Essay

1. a. The Latin word *exponere* literally means to *set forth*. The purpose of the **expository essay** is to set forth information and explain a given topic. Although a writer may add his personal feelings on the topic, the facts are central to the essay.

   You have probably written a biography or research paper. These are examples of expository essays. Read the sample expository essay found on the following page.

   b. The structure of the sample expository essay consists of:
   1) **introductory paragraph**
   2) three **body paragraphs**
   3) **concluding paragraph**

   The length of the essay is between five and six hundred words, which is average for this style of essay. The introductory and concluding paragraphs are a little different than the body paragraphs. To gain insight into essay structure, let's examine the body paragraphs first:

   The first body paragraph (second paragraph of the essay) follows a definite pattern. It consists of a **topic sentence**, three **subtopics**, and **concluding sentences**. The topic, which is "the scholar's attitude towards school," tells us that the scholar takes academics seriously. Under this topic are three subtopics. First are the scholar's study habits (sentences 2-4), then his social life (sentences 5-7), and then his appearance (sentences 8-9). The last two sentences make conclusions about this type of person based on the information given. Within each subtopic there are specific examples to illustrate the point. We are not merely told that the scholar studies hard, we are given specific examples of how this is accomplished. These kinds of details bring expository writing to life. Most students can create an outline, but writing skill generally varies according to one's ability to provide specific examples which bring the topic and subtopics to clarity.

   It may be helpful to think of the body paragraph as a miniature of the overall essay form. There is an **introduction**, three **subtopics**, and a **conclusion**. If you follow this pattern, you will keep your essays from getting out of balance or off topic.

Types of College Students

College can be a place where vague hopes become concrete realities. The romantic notions of adolescence are gradually abandoned for the sobering responsibilities of training for an adult career. Most universities provide a broad range of educational opportunities which attract an equally diverse student enrollment. Although students vary greatly in appearance, background, and intelligence, they may be grouped with regard to their attitudes toward school as the scholar, the student, and the pupil.

The scholar's attitude toward school is slanted always in favor of academics. He studies at the library between classes and occupies his evenings at the desk in the dorm room. Whether he is memorizing names and dates for history or puzzling over a math theorem, he will take time to thoroughly prepare for class. The scholar's high grades reflect his dedication to excellence. Often he must achieve such results at the expense of other activities, including social forays. While others participate in activities, the scholar only studies and takes care of necessary survival items such as eating and resting. This is not to say he is socially inept – he merely chooses to sacrifice pleasure for academic goals. One cannot discern a scholar at first glance. He might be dressed in old jeans and a tee-shirt or he could be attired with an Izod™ shirt and Calvin Klein™ jeans. Regardless, this student type is willing to make short-term sacrifices for long-term goals. His employment statistics after graduation are marked by high achievement as well.

For the student type, academics are highly important but not all consuming. This person always does his homework, but seldom pursues anything outside the assigned material. He makes time to study as needed, meeting the demands of the assignment. Although the student will not accept less than a C, he works for A's only to demonstrate that he can make them. The student's approach to social life is the same as his approach to schoolwork. Football games, weekend parties, and organizations are important to the one who needs to relax and return to academics refreshed. Recognizing that socializing is important in one's career, the student complements his education with these equally practical developments of his character. In keeping with his practicality, his dress is stylish but functional. With well trimmed hair and a *carefully washed face, he is always ready for social interaction. These people are in great demand by businesses, churches, and suburban neighborhoods.*

The pupil's attitude toward school is to get by with the minimum effort. Perhaps they are the ones who created the slogan "Get your 2.0 and go." Regardless, these student types survive academically, but are not serious about excelling. The pupil's social life is equally unambitious. For him, fraternities require too much effort and involvement. He prefers to take his social life spontaneously, making it up as he goes along, letting it unfold without working at it. If nothing unfolds, a night of television watching will do. The pupil's dress code also reflects a cavalier attitude. Choosing his wardrobe easily, he selects from jeans, pull-over shirts, sweat socks and anything else which can be thrown in the washer all at once and dried without ironing. Perhaps there is something to be admired about the pupils because they seem to be so relaxed about things that one never suspects they may have sleepless nights or ulcers.

Depending on attitudes and goals, each student assumes some characteristics of one of the three subclasses. Scholars, with their tendency to exclude all but academics, are perhaps too confined to their studies to be truly well-rounded. The pupils and their debased activities are not suitable for acceptable inclusion in adult society. However, the students, with their well-rounded social and academic backgrounds, undoubtedly are the most well prepared for success as our society defines it.

c. An outline of the paragraph about the scholar (paragraph 2) might look like this:

I. The scholar's attitude toward school is seriously academic.

II. Study habits

    A. studies at the library

    B. studies between classes

    C. studies at home

    D. prepares for class

    E. memorizes materials

    F. dedicated to excellence

III. Social life

    A. puts social life aside

    B. no parties

    C. tends to basic needs only

    D. sacrifices pleasure for academics

IV. Appearance

    A. you can't tell a scholar at first glance

    B. he might be sloppy

    C. he might be preppie

V. He makes short-term sacrifices for long term goals. These people are hired by the best employers.

a. Two important factors to remember when writing an essay are unity and coherence. The paragraphs in the sample essay are tight. Every sentence in each paragraph relates back to the topic and develops it in some way.

Coherence is provided by the author's skill in relating one sentence to the next. He does this by the use of transitional devices. **Transitional words** relate one sentence to the next. In paragraph two, the author used transitional words sparingly and chose to relate sentences by associating information from sentence to sentence. For example, we know that sentence two follows coherently because *he* relates back to *scholar*. The same is true of sentence three. Then *scholar* is restated in sentence four.

Furthermore (furthermore is a transitional word, by the way), the writer repeats information such as academics, studies, memorizing, puzzling, prepare, etc. Get the point? We need to be advised, as readers, that one sentence relates to the next. This is often accomplished by transitional words or phrases such as:

furthermore	moreover	for example
in contrast	to illustrate	in addition
first	finally	second
next	therefore	similarly

There are numerous transitional words and phrases. The point is that they are necessary in giving the reader clues to follow your train of thought.

b. Read the introductory paragraph again. This, too, is very skillfully written. Rather than being concerned with subtopics at this point, the writer has started with a very general statement, and gradually narrowed it down to a very specific topic for the essay. This is called the **thesis statement**. The thesis statement is usually the last sentence in the introductory paragraph, and tells the reader the topic of the essay. A good thesis statement is clear and concise. As is the case here, the thesis often announces the paragraph topics as well. Once the thesis is stated, all further information relates back to it in one way or another. The thesis is the controlling point of the essay from which all else follows. The thesis statement is reworded in the concluding paragraph.

c. Read the concluding paragraph of the sample essay again. This is superb. The author generally summarizes the main points of the essay, and makes a concluding statement. This is a reworded thesis statement. He uses the information in the paper to go beyond the facts and makes an analysis. This is a fine conclusion, and shows us a reason for classifying the student types. Perhaps the well-rounded person described here might be a reminder to all of us not to be too out of balance in any area.

3. a. Now that we have examined the writing process for the essay, you will begin your essay. Choose an essay topic from the novels or short stories you have read. For example, an often examined essay topic for *The Old Man and the Sea* is Santiago as a Christ figure. Although we know that Santiago is not a Christ-like character, there is a good deal of Christ-like imagery surrounding him. Perhaps we might modify our topic to be, "The Imagery of Christ Surrounding the Character of Santiago."

   Once we have our thesis, then it must be supported with evidence from the story: author interpretations, dialogue, descriptions, actions.

   Begin your outline.

   Look at the following outline guide for an essay.

   I.   Introduction
   II. Subtopic
        A. Supporting detail
        B. Supporting detail
   III. Subtopic
        A. Supporting detail
        B. Supporting detail
   IV. Subtopic
        A. Supporting detail
        B. Supporting detail
   V.   Conclusion

4. a. Using your outline, begin a **rough draft** on your expository essay. What remains, now, is to flesh out the paragraphs with imaginative details to illustrate the points. It is often easier to begin with the body paragraphs. Add the introduction and conclusion later. Allow several days to work on your rough draft.

   b. Edit your paper for grammar, punctuation, and spelling. Write your **final draft**.

c. This is a sample outline for *The Old Man and the Sea.*

I. The imagery of Christ surrounding the character of Santiago
II. Santiago's physical sufferings
   A. rope striped back
   B. bleeding hands
   C. general agony
III. Harpoon in the marlin's side
   A. Santiago identifies with the fish
   B. he says he is the fish
   C. he wishes he were the fish
IV. Santiago struggles to carry the mast
   A. mast is cross-shaped
   B. like Christ, he collapses several times
   C. last state of his ordeal is like the final steps of Jesus
V. Santiago portrays Christ-like images

Essay Assessment I

To help you assess your student's essay, complete the following checklist.

The essay contains:

1) a thesis statement that clearly identifies the main idea _____

2) an introductory paragraph _____

3) body paragraphs that support the main idea _____

4) a concluding paragraph _____

5) a topic sentence for each paragraph _____

6) sentences within a paragraph that relate back to the topic sentence _____

7) transitional words to relate one sentence to the next _____

8) a reworded thesis statement in the concluding paragraph _____

9) cohesiveness and unity _____

10) correct grammar, punctuation, and spelling _____

If your student has missed any of the above points, encourage him to go back and improve his essay. Congratulate him for his effort and completion.

UNIT 4

Poetry

For The Poetry Unit, you will read the following poems from *Th Mentor Book of Major American Poets*, edited by Oscar Williams and Edwin Honig, published by Penguin Group ISBN 0-451-62791-1.

The Snowstorm	by Ralph Waldo
Concord Hymn	Emerson
Fable	
Good-bye	
The Day is Done	by Henry Wadsworth
Evangeline	Longfellow
The Song of Hiawatha	
Because I Could Not Stop for Death	by Emily Dickinson
Success is Counted Sweetest	
A Bird Came Down the Walk	
I Taste a Liquor Never Brewed	
Cliff Klingenhagen	by Edwin Arlington
Bewick Finzer	Robinson
Fleming Helphenstine	
In the Desert	by Stephen Crane
A Learned Man Came to Me Once	
The Impact of a Dollar	
Mending Wall	by Robert Frost
Stopping by Woods on a Snowy Evening	
Birches	
The Road Not Taken	
Queen-Ann's-Lace	by William Carlos
The Dance	Williams
By the Road to the Contagious Hospital	

The Poetry Unit

Read the objectives with your student. New literary terms should be added to the student's notebook in section three. A list of the terms is provided following the objectives. *Words to Know* appear throughout the poetry section and include definitions. The student can add these to his notebook in section two for vocabulary if you wish. The writing assignments and poems the student will be writing are added to section one.

Objectives

1) to acquaint the student to American poets and their poetry
2) to understand the various poetic styles and techniques
3) to help the student analyze and interpret poetry
4) to enhance the student's appreciation for poetry
5) to encourage the student to write his own poetry

Terms to Identify

personification
rhyme scheme
simile
imagery
metaphor
implied metaphor
sonnet
iambic foot
metrical pattern
iambic pentameter
octave
quatrain
sestet
tercet
stanza
abstractions
concrete
blank verse
free verse
symbol
syntax

Poetry is difficult and frustrating to understand at times, but it is not impossible. With a little guidance and a good deal of study, its mysteries can be unraveled. If you go slowly, and concentrate, the poems should unfold, and the efforts you make will seem worthwhile and satisfying.

Most textbooks which contain a unit on poetry explains the mechanics of poetry, such as rhyme, meter, rhyme scheme, etc. Learning Language Arts Through Literature, *The Green Book*, contains a unit on poetry which teaches these elements of craft more extensively. Any references in this section to rhyme and meter, etc., which might need to be reviewed, can be done by referring to *The Green Book* or another suitable reference.

The goal of this section is to derive an understanding of how to read a poem for its content. The selections are taken from American poets and cover a time period from about 1800-1960. During this period, the form of poetry changed, and we can follow this development.

Read each poem several times before answering any questions. When you complete the assigned poems, you may choose several other poems by the same poet to read and discuss with your teacher.

Page numbers refer to the poetry selections found in *The Mentor Book of Major American Poets*, edited by Oscar Williams and Edwin Honig, Penguin Books, ISBN 0-451-62791-1.

Poet's Corner

Ralph Waldo Emerson (1803-1882) was born in Boston from a long line of ministers. Although his father died when Ralph was a young boy, his mother's hard work and strong will enabled him and his brothers to finish college. After graduating from Harvard, he went to divinity school. He became the pastor of the Second Church of Boston, but due to doctrinal differences, Emerson left his church and went to Europe. There, he became acquainted with Coleridge, Wordsworth, and other British writers. He later returned home and settled in Concord, Massachusetts.

Emerson is well known for his philosophy of transcendentalism, the idea that the search for truth may be found through nature and spiritual intuition. He was known as the "Sage of Concord" and was deeply respected and sought after as an intellectual and lecturer. However, he was more drawn to the quietness of his own home. At his death, he was buried in Concord in Sleepy Hollow Cemetery.

1. a. Read "The Snowstorm" found on page 51.

    b. Words to know:

        1) Parian - a type of porcelain
        2) maugre - in spite of
        3) tumultuous - violently agitated
        4) artificer - a skilled craftsman
        5) bastions - the projecting parts of a fort
        6) myriad - innumerable
        7) turret - a tower

    c. Poets use figurative language to create imagery and emotion in their writing. Common figures of speech are personification, simile, and metaphor. In this poem, Emerson uses personification. **Personification** is a figure of speech which gives human attributes to something that is not human. We can personify inanimate objects, plants, animals or even abstract concepts such as death. Emerson uses personification in this poem to bring the wind to life. To what does Emerson compare the wind?

In his journal, dated November 27, 1832, he writes: "Instead of lectures on architecture, I will make a lecture on God's architecture, one of his beautiful works, a day. I will draw a sketch of a winter's day. I will trace as I can a rude outline of the far-assembled influences, the contribution of the universe wherein this magical structure rises like an exhalation, the wonder and charm of the immeasurable deep."

d. What are some words or phrases he uses to convey the image of the wind?

e. What is the mood of the poem? What do you envision, and how does it make you feel?

f. Write a poem using personification to illustrate an element of nature.

2. a. Read "Concord Hymn" found on page 44.

b. The Battle of Concord was fought on April 19, 1775. Emerson commemorated the battle with the Concord Hymn which was sung at the completion of the Battle Monument on July 4, 1837 in Concord.

 The first stanza describes the setting. To what do you think their *flag to April's breeze unfurled* refers?

c. What does *the shot heard round the world* mean?

d. What do you think is the significance of the fourth stanza?

🖉 **Teacher Note: Activities for Day 2 are continued on the next page.**

e. The **rhyme scheme** of a poem is the pattern of rhyme at the end of lines. Rhyme schemes are noted by designating small letters for each rhyming pattern. For example, look at the following lines from Emerson's "The Humblebee" found on page 45.

Burly, dozing humblebee,
Where thou art is clime for me.
Let them sail for Porto Rique,
Far-off heats through seas to seek;
I will follow thee alone,
Thou animated torrid zone!
Zigzag steerer, desert cheerer,
Let me chase thy waving lines;
Keep me nearer, me thy hearer,
Singing over shrubs and vines.

The end words *humbleblee* and *me* rhyme, so we designate the letter **a**. The end words *Rique* and *seek* rhyme, so we designate the letter **b**. The end words *alone* and *zone* rhyme, so we designate the letter **c**. If we continue in this manner, the rhyme scheme of the poem is **aabbccdede**.

What is the rhyme scheme of "Concord Hymn"?

f. Write a short poem and determine its rhyme scheme.

3. a. Read "Fable" found on page 51.
   Emerson included this poem in his *Selected Poems* published in 1876.

b. Why do you think Emerson titled this poem "Fable"?

c. What do you think the poem means?

d. Try writing a fable poem of your own.

4. a. Read "Good-bye" found on page 62.
   A note of interest is the history behind the word *good-bye*. It became a shortened form of the phrase *God be with you.*

b. What is the rhyme scheme in "Good-bye"?

c. The mood of a poem arouses feelings in the reader. What is the mood of this poem?

d. To what or to whom was the poet saying good-bye?

e. Read the last two lines of the poem again. Where does the poet believe one can find God?

Do you agree or disagree? Defend your position.

f. What does the poem mean to you? Write a few sentences or draw a picture depicting the feelings which were aroused.

a. Look over the poetry you read this week. Choose two or three poems for an oral recitation.

b. Read each poem several times. When you are ready, read the poems to your teacher, family, or class.

1.

c. Emerson compares the wind to an artificer, a skilled craftsman.

d. north wind's masonry; curves his white bastions; his wild work so fanciful; a tapering turret; architecture of the snow

e. The mood is quiet, cold, and calming.

Answers will vary.

2.

b. It refers to the soldier's flag blowing in April, the month of the battle.

c. It was the first shot of the battle; it symbolizes freedom.

d. Emerson is asking God to remember the dead soldiers.

e. The rhyme scheme of "Concord Hymn" is abab abab abab abab.

3.

b. It is akin to fables such as those that Aesop wrote, teaching a truth in a simple manner.

c. The small and the big are both parts of the whole, each having its purpose.

4.

b. ababaa aabbccde aabbccdd aabbccdd

c. It is rather somber and serious.

d. He was dismayed and was saying good-bye to the worldliness he saw around him, the pride of learned men, etc.

e. in nature

Answers will vary.

f. Answers will vary.

Poet's Corner

Henry Wadsworth Longfellow (1807-1882) was born in the busy seaport of Portland, Maine. The excitement and blend of people of the harbors provided Henry with a rich experience. From a very early age, Henry was drawn to writing. He was greatly inspired by Washington Irving's *Sketch Book*.

As a young man he went to Europe to study as a linguist. He had opportunities to meet distinguished men and women of England and France. But he found he enjoyed the simple life in the countryside. There, he befriended peasants and farmers. He returned to America a few years later and began his professorship. He married, but his wife died a few years later. Years later, Longfellow remarried. He established a happy home with five children. After resigning from Harvard, he took on the sole task of writing poetry, his great joy. Longfellow received honorary degrees at Oxford and Cambridge Universities.

Of all the American poets, Longfellow is probably one the best loved. When the day came to cut down the tree which Longfellow referred to as "the spreading chestnut tree" in his poem, "Village Blacksmith," the children of Cambridge had it made into a chair and gave it to Longfellow as a gift. He died in 1882 in Cambridge, Massachusetts. He was honored two years later with a bust which was placed in the Poet's Corner of Westminster Abbey. He was the first American to receive this recognition. Longfellow's poetry is full of beauty, marked with easy rhyme. They are basically easy to understand and leave the reader with a joyful, melodic spirit.

1. a. Read "The Day is Done" found on page 65.

   b. The **simile** is another common poetic device. It is a type of figurative language which makes a comparison between two things by using words such as *like*, *as*, *appears*, and *seems*. What is the simile in the first stanza?

      How does Longfellow use the simile effectively?

   c. Find the simile in the third stanza.

      How does Longfellow use the simile to express his feelings?

d. Find the simile in the seventh stanza.

Do you think this simile is effective? Why?

e. Find the similes in the ninth and last stanza.

f. Write a poem using similes to create vivid pictures and evoke emotion.

2. a. Read "Evangeline" found on page 86.
   Note: This is only part of the long narrative poem.

   b. Words to Know:
      1) Grand-Pré - French, meaning great meadow
      2) primeval - primitive
      3) Druids - priests of a Celtic religious order
      4) eld - ancient times
      5) hoar - very old
      6) disconsolate - not to be comforted

   c. The meaning of this poem will be gained with a little background knowledge of the Acadians. Using your library or reference books, find out some information about these people.

3. a. Read "The Song of Hiawatha" found on page 87.
   Note: This is only part of the long narrative poem.

   Longfellow was one of the first Americans to write about the Native American people. When "The Song of Hiawatha" was published in 1855, it was an instant success. Although the real Hiawatha was an Iroquois chief during the late 1500's, Longfellow's Hiawatha is from the Ojibwa tribe. Legend tells that he was raised by his grandmother, Nokomis, and he learned to talk to the animals and the forest. He exceeded in all the manly skills and grew up to be a leader. He married the fair maiden Minnehaha and became the peacemaker among neighboring tribes.

   b. This poem is enjoyable to read aloud. Practice reading it aloud on your own, and then find an audience to read to. Have fun.

4-5. Use the next two days to read more poetry by Longfellow, and write your own poetry.

1.

b. ... the darkness falls...as a
   feather is wafted downward

   The darkness falls softly and
   gradually like a feather.

c. A feeling of sadness and
   longing... as the mist resembles
   the rain.

   The sadness isn't a deep pain
   but a heaviness of heart.

d. ... songs...as showers from the
   clouds of summer or tears from
   the eyelids...

   Yes. Just as summer clouds get
   so full that a burst of showers
   breaks forth, so is the song in a
   poet's heart.

e. ninth stanza: songs... like the
   benediction
   last stanza: night... like the
   Arabs

2.

c. When disputes arose between
   the French settlers and British
   colonists, the Acadians wanted
   to continue their peaceful farm
   life. The Acadians were
   originally from France. They did
   not want to take an oath of
   allegiance to England and
   wished to be excused from
   warring against the French.
   Therefore, the Acadians were
   deported and settled in various
   states. This caused the
   separation of family and friends.
   In this poem, Longfellow tells a
   sad love story of the separation
   of Evangeline and Gabriel.

Poet's Corner

Emily Elizabeth Dickinson was born in Amherst, Massachusetts on December 10, 1830. She was reared in a puritan home with a father who governed his family with authority and expected his children to heed his religious beliefs without thought.

As a young girl, Emily was active, happy, and outgoing. By her midtwenties, she began to withdraw from public life. She tended to her domestic chores and her poetry. She admired the poetry of Robert and Elizabeth Barrett Browning and John Keats.

During her forties, Emily became more reclusive. She wore white gowns and rarely went out. Emily never married, but she had a few significant relationships. The later years of her life brought much grief with the death of several loved ones.

Emily wrote about 2,000 poems, but only a handful were published during her lifetime. Her poems mostly deal with nature, love, death, and humanity. Her poems are generally short and most are untitled.

On May 15, 1886, Emily Dickinson, one of the first truly great American poets, died from her illness of Bright's disease.

1. a. Read "Because I Could Not Stop for Death" found on page 199.

   b. Words to know:
      1) civility - courtesy
      2) gossamer - fine, silky threads
      3) tippet - a long scarf or shawl
      4) tulle - a thin, fine net-like fabric
      5) cornice - the projection at the top of a building
      6) surmised - concluded

   c. Why do you think the poet "could not stop for death"?

   d. How does Dickinson personify death? Give examples from the poem.

e. There are at least three other personifications in the poem besides death. They are not as obvious, but read the poem again and try to find them. Once you find them, the clues to their identities will stand out.

f. Dickinson did not title most of her poems. As the poems were published, the first line of the poems were added as titles. Think of a suitable title for this poem.

g. In the fifth stanza, to what do you think the house refers?

h. Although the subject of the poem is death, what is the mood of the poem?

i. Draw a picture depicting the mood of the poem.

Write a poem using personification. Use something you are personally familiar with and personify that object.

Suggestions:
a new car or an old shoe
the teddy bear in a corner of your closet, long forgotten and
    feeling like someone who's been robbed, beaten, and
    thrown on the side of the road
your baseball glove, like an old friend
the tree out back that watched you grow up

a. Read the poem "Success is Counted Sweetest" found on page 186.

b. Briefly describe what the poem is about.

c. Dickinson conveys that those who took the flag cannot tell the definition of victory, but the defeated can. Why do you think so?

d. Do you agree with the poet's thoughts on success? Write two to three paragraphs on what success means to you.

a. Read "A Bird Came Down the Walk" found on page 192.

b. Briefly describe what the poem is about.

c. Compare the first three stanzas with the last two stanzas. How has the poet's perspective of the bird changed from t beginning of the poem to the end of the poem?

d. Compare yesterday's poem, "Success is Counted Sweetest," with "A Bird Came Down the Walk." Which poem has the more substantial subject matter?

e. In comparing these two poems, notice that "Success is Counted Sweetest" merely tells us in direct language what are supposed to think. "A Bird Came Down the Walk," however, unfolds with many images for us to see, and we a shown rather than told what to think. This goes back to the old refrain among creative writers that you will hear in all t workshops, whether they are poetry or fiction workshops: show us, don't tell us. Notice how Dickinson takes something as insignificant as encountering a bird, yet magnifies it into an entire poem. She does this with a great building block of poetry: **imagery**. She draws picture afte picture for us, until our senses are full by the end of the poem; whereas "Success is Counted Sweetest" is proverbia and rather more like an essay than a poem. A point often overlooked by readers is that images can involve all five senses. Thus, the poet wants to invoke taste, smell, touch, and hearing, in addition to the visual, and we must be alert these possibilities for imagery.

Compare "Success is Counted Sweetest" with "A Bird Cam Down the Walk." Which one do you think is more poetic?

f. Write a poem using imagery.

5. a. Read "I Taste a Liquor Never Brewed" found on page 188.

b. Words to know:
    1) tankards - a large drinking cup with a handle, often with hinged lid
    2) inebriate - to make drunk
    3) debauchee - one who indulges in sensual pleasures
    4) renounce - to give up
    5) dram(s) - a small drink of alcoholic liquor
    6) tippler - one who drinks alcoholic liquor habitually
    7) manzanilla - a dry Spanish sherry

c. One of the keys to understanding poetry is to understand metaphor. A **metaphor** is a comparison between two things which are not usually thought to be related. For example, Shakespeare writes, "life...is a brief candle." Some metaphors are **implied**; the comparison is never stated, and the reader is expected to recognize it without being told, such as "hearts of stone."

A common metaphor runs through the entire poem. What is it?

d. Imagery is often achieved through the use of figurative language such as personification, metaphors, similes, and analogies.

What is the liquor in line one, which she refers to again as alcohol in line four?

e. Consider the phrases *inebriate of air* and *debauchee of dew*. To what is *air* and *dew* compared?

f. What do these comparisons suggest about Dickinson's appreciation for air and dew?

g. What are the *inns of molten blue*, and how does this metaphor contribute to Dickinson's mood?

h. There is another metaphor in stanza three. Find the metaphor and try to explain it. Let me give you a hint: A bee can be drunk just like any other animal. Drunken bee, therefore, is not a metaphor.

i. Who is the *little tippler* in line thirteen?

j. Is the little tippler being compared to anything else in the poem?

k. Talk with your teacher about an experience you had which relates to the joy of being in God's creation. Jot down your thoughts. Try writing a short poem about creation.

1.

c. Death is inevitable.

d. Dickinson creates a kindly, considerate person to represent death.
"He kindly stopped for me" - kind
"He knew no haste" - patient
"For his civility" - considerate

e. These are rather obscure personifications compared to Death, but they're legitimate, nevertheless.
Line four - Immortality is another rider in the carriage. (Some manuscripts capitalize immortality, giving a further clue to its personification.)
Line eleven - the grain is gazing
Line thirteen - the sun is referred to as a he who passes the carriage

f. Answers will vary.

g. Possible answer: a grave

h. serene and peaceful

2. Allow for creativity.

3.

b. The poem is about the tendency for people to desire most the things which they haven't attained, but think they would like to.

c. Just as "success is counted sweetest by those who never succeed," victory is known by the defeated.

d. Answers will vary.

4.

b. It is about the poet's encounter with a bird as she was taking a walk.

c. Possible answer: The first three stanzas convey the bird as just something to amuse you. The last two stanzas convey the bird as an object of beauty and grace.

d. "Success is Counted Sweetest" is almost philosophical, whereas "A Bird Came Down the Walk" is trivial in comparison.

e. "Success is Counted Sweetest" is almost prosaic. It has very little poetic merit, whereas "A Bird Came Down the Walk" is loaded with imaginative language.

5.

c. Being inebriated with alcohol is compared to being enraptured with creation.

d. She is intoxicated with nature.

e. Air and dew are compared to alcoholic beverages.

f. She is saying that things such as morning air and dew are exhilarating and make the head swim.

g. The inns of molten blue conjure up an image of blue waters. This excitement perhaps makes her head swim.

h. The foxglove is compared to a dwelling: It has a door, and is supervised by a landlord. This is a comparison of a place in the sky where sustenance and lodging are found which covers the earth like a roof, and therefore covers nature, which is the ultimate source for food and lodging.

i. the bee

j. yes — Dickinson

Poet's Corner

Edwin Arlington Robinson was born in 1869 in Head Tide, Maine. He grew up in Gardiner, Maine and attended Harvard University. Upon moving to New York, he continued to struggle with his poetry until his volume, *Captain Craig and Other Poems*, came to the favorable attention of President Theodore Roosevelt. After receiving national recognition, he continued to succeed, winning three Pulitzer Prizes during his career. He is perhaps best known for his *Tilbury Poems*, poetry set in an imaginary town modeled after Gardiner, his childhood home. He died in 1935.

. a. Read "Cliff Klingenhagen" found on page 211.

   b. Words to know:
   1) wormwood - generally, a bitter or unpleasant experience
   2) draught - a dose of liquid
   3) quaffed - drank deeply in a hearty manner
   4) deuce - an exclamation of annoyance

   c. How many lines are in the poem, "Cliff Klingenhagen"?

"Cliff Klingenhagen" is an example of a strict form of poetry called a **sonnet**. A sonnet usually consists of fourteen lines, and is usually written in iambic pentameter.

Look at the first two lines of "Cliff Klingenhagen." Note the pattern which consists of one unstressed and one stressed syllable. This is called an **iambic foot**. The type of feet and number of lines determine the **metrical pattern** of a poem.

  ᴜ / ᴜ / ᴜ / ᴜ / ᴜ /
Cliff Klingenhagen had me in to dine

  ᴜ / ᴜ / ᴜ /ᴜ / ᴜ   /
With him one day; and after soup and meat,

This poem consists of five iambic feet per line. This metrical pattern is called an **iambic pentameter**.

   d. Determine the rhyme scheme of "Cliff Klingenhagen."

   e. The lines of this poem and other sonnets have a strict rhyme scheme of **abba, acca, def, def**. The first eight lines of a sonnet (**abba, acca**) are called the **octave**. The octave can b further divided in half to form two **quatrains**.

f.   The last six lines (**def, def**) are called the **sestet**. The sestet can also be divided in half to form two **tercets**.

These divisions are like **stanzas**, a grouping of lines set off b a space, usually following a pattern of meter and rhyme. Each stanza is like a paragraph which develops a topic.

g.   Using today's poem, read the octave and the sestet separately Why do you think there is such a difference between the rhyme schemes of the octave and sestet?

h.   Sometimes there is a difference in content between the first and second quatrains of a sonnet. However, Robinson does not differentiate between the two. How do we know this?

i.   Look at the sestet. Is there a difference between the first an second tercets?

j.   Notice how the structure of the sonnet, being divided into octave and two tercets, gives clues to the content of the poen Be alert to signals such as rhyme groups and stanza breaks which show us that a new topic has begun. These structural devices are like paragraphs, and are keys to unraveling the content of a poem.

The octave of "Cliff Klingenhagen" is like an introductory paragraph in which Robinson provides a little scene for us tc think about. Summarize, in two or three sentences, what happens in this scene.

k.   How does the first tercet add to the meaning of the octave?

l.   The last tercet shows the narrator of the poem reflecting about what has happened. Why do you think Cliff Klingenhagen is so happy? Write down a few sentences explaining why you think Cliff is happy.

m. Today begin writing a sonnet. You may take some time the next two days to work on it, too.

a. Read "Bewick Finzer" found on page 212.

b. Words to know:
   1) credence - belief
   2) indigence - the condition of being poor
   3) imponderable - that cannot be explained
   4) affluence - an abundance of wealth

c. What is the rhyme scheme of the first two stanzas of "Bewick Finzer"?

d. How many syllables per line are there in the first two stanzas?

e. Although this poem has a regular pattern among its stanzas, it does not conform to any existing form, and appears to be Robinson's own invention. We can make two conclusions about this. First, the form of the poem doesn't give many clues to its content. Secondly, it is acceptable for a poet to experiment with forms and create his own forms.

f. "Bewick Finzer" is typical of many of Robinson's poems, in which he sketches a character for us, and then lets us draw our own conclusions about what the character shows us.

   In stanzas three and four, Robinson uses numerous descriptions of Finzer's outward appearance and physical actions to support the last two lines of stanza one. Find the physical images that show us Finzer's fallen condition. Explain how the physical descriptions, each in its own way, show us a different aspect of Finzer's condition.

g. Do you find these physical descriptions effective? Do you think we would still understand the meaning of the poem without stanzas three and four?

h. What does the poem mean to you?

i. If you need to, complete the sonnet you began yesterday.

3. a. Read "Fleming Helphenstine" found on page 211.

    b. The first quatrain describes Helphenstine's face. Remembe[r]
        the quatrain is the first four lines of the octave. (See **1e**.)
        Judging by his face, what kind of fellow is he?

        What does the second quatrain tell us about Helphenstine?

    c. Now that Robinson has sketched a character for us, we are
        ready to examine the sestet.

        What image in the ninth line shows us that there is a comp[lete]
        change in Helphenstine's attitude?

        What do *frown*, *gazed*, and *wince* all have in common?

    d. We are not told why Helphenstine suddenly closes himself
        and goes away, but there is plenty of evidence that suggests [a]
        reason. Reread the octave and see if you can think of a
        reason.

    e. Do you think there is such a thing as being too open? Have
        you ever told someone something about yourself and that
        person later used it against you? Do you have close friends
        with whom you can share your most carefully kept secrets?
        Do you find this healthful? Do you share your intimate
        feelings with your parents?
        Ponder these questions, discuss with your teacher, or write
        a personal journal.

    f. If you need to, complete the sonnet you began in **1m**.

4-5. Enjoy these two days immersing yourself in poetry. If yo[u]
      can, find someone to read the poetry with you. Discuss
      what they mean to you. Poetry is written to be shared wi[th]
      others.

14 lines

abba acca def def

There is a change in the subject matter and therefore the meanings of the two.

The sentence beginning in line four runs over to line five connecting the quatrains.

Here, there is a clear difference between the two tercets.

Mr. Klingenhagen had a visitor over for dinner one night. After dinner, he got out two glasses, filling one with wormwood and the other with wine. Mr. Klingenhagen drank the wormwood and offered his visitor the wine.

This is apparently not the first time Klingenhagen has done this. He does it habitually, and probably does this with other things besides after-dinner drinks.

Klingenhagen takes pleasure in seeing to the welfare of others, even to his own disadvantage. He has become accustomed to unselfishness, and therefore is much more content with what he has, and probably doesn't worry about how things could be better.

abcbdb, efgfhf

Stanza 1: 8, 6, 8, 6, 8, 6
Stanza 2: 8, 6, 8, 6, 8, 6

broken voice - suggests a difficulty with speech that could have been brought on by emotional devastation, poor health, or both

withered neck - suggests that he has aged considerably and may not eat very well
coat worn out - shows us his low economic status and excessive anxiety, as the rest of the line implies

g. Yes. We know the meaning of the poem from the first two stanzas, but the images in three and four make Finzer's condition real to us. They add to the poem by showing us how far he has fallen.

h. Possible answer: When our self-worth depends on our money and possessions, it is a fragile, superficial thing.

3.
b. The first quatrain shows us a happy, outgoing fellow.

The second quatrain tells us that he is a stranger, but takes on a familiarity with other people. Apparently his conversation is a little superficial, and he seems to presume that a stranger will be interested.

c. The frown indicates that Helphenstine is suddenly displeased about something.

These three words are all facial expressions with negative associations. Even *gazed*, in this context, has a negative tone to it.

d. He realizes he has made himself vulnerable to a stranger. The narrator doesn't seem too interested, as line seven suggests.

e. Allow for discussion.

Poet's Corner

Stephen Crane (1871-1900) lived to be only 29 years old, but he left a significant mark in American literature. His short novel, *The Red Badge of Courage*, earned him international acclaim at the age of 24. Crane was deeply affected by the harsh realities of war. He continued writing until his death.

Stephen Crane's marvelous fiction ensures his place among the world's immortal writers. However, his poetry was not very good, and there are a few observations to be made.

1. a. Read "In the Desert" found on page 224.

   b. Read line two. What does the creature look like?

      Words such as *creature* and *bestial* are called **abstractions**. This means they are generalities which have no specific meaning. Poets should avoid abstractions and give specific details that show us what he wants us to know. In line two Crane should have given this creature a good physical description. Try your hand at line two.

   c. The words *heart*, *good*, and even the word *bitter* are abstractions in this poem. Consider each word, and explain why they are abstractions.

   d. This entire poem is symbolic, meaning it has another meaning other than its literal one. (The use of a **symbol** will be further discussed in Lesson 28.) What do you think is the meaning of the poem?

      We have no idea why the creature is eating his heart. There can be any number of reasons, and it is the poet's job to give us a reason. For example, in "Bewick Finzer," we know that his condition results from a concrete fact: He lost all his money. Crane, however, does not provide a clue as to the reason for the creature's condition. Therefore, we really have no idea what the creature's attitude actually is.

   e. The opposite of abstract is **concrete**. Something is concrete if it is specific. When writing poetry, concrete words create

images. Remember, images can involve any of the senses: taste, smell, touch, hearing, and of course visual.
Try writing a poem, avoiding the abstract.

2. a. Read "A Learned Man Came to Me Once" found on page 225.

   b. What do you think Crane means by *the way* in line two?

       What does he mean by the phrase *I am lost* in the last line?

   c. One of the most frequent misconceptions among beginning poets is the belief that a poem should consist of generalizations and abstractions so that the reader can fill in his own details. Just the opposite is true of good poetry. The more specific and concrete the poem is, the more the reader can identify with its message.

       Here is a common list of abstractions to avoid when writing poetry: good, honest, true, sincere, beauty, heart, love, warmth, trust, evil, hate, secure.

       Make a list of abstractions of your own.

   d. Write another poem today. Remember to avoid abstracts.

3. a. Read "The Impact of a Dollar" found on page 233.

   b. Words to know:
       1) flunkies - flattering people seeking attention
       2) emblems - a representation or symbol of some invisible quality, idea, or thought
       3) cryptic - mysterious
       4) baubles - showy but worthless things
       5) champing - biting repeatedly and restlessly

   c. What are the abstractions in the first two lines?

   d. What does the first stanza mean to you?

   e. Does the second stanza clarify the meaning? Explain.

4. a. Read one or two more of Stephen Crane's poetry of your choice.

   b. Today, we will continue the lesson of avoiding abstractions. Consider the word *love*, for example. If we have the line "I love you," and follow this with a few lines comparing this love with the sky, sea, etc., the problem with abstract language becomes apparent. First, we cannot assume that the object of such love is romantic. I love my children in a much different way than I love my wife. I love my friends differently from my family.

   Neither philosophers nor the Bible has ever defined love. St. Paul, for instance, gives some characteristics of love, but does not give a comprehensive list, nor does he define it. (Refer to I Cor. 13.) Therefore, modern poets do not use the word love — they give an illustration that shows us an aspect of love. Consequently, the "love" poem might record excerpts of a conversation over dinner, or might describe an intimacy over dinner that was communicated without conversation. Regardless, it is the poet's job to describe the experience of love by showing us one of the limitless situations in which love is communicated. However, this must be done with concrete details in which the word *love* cannot be used.

   c. Write a "love" poem to your mother and/or your father. Try to choose an incident or incidents that best describes the love that you feel. Remember to show how your love is demonstrated. This will take some thought.

5. Write another "love" poem to your brother, sister, or anyone else of your choice.

We don't know. We know
nothing of its appearance — not
the slightest detail.

These words cannot be seen,
tasted, etc. They cannot be
defined. They are vague and
formless.

Answers will vary greatly
because the poem is too
abstract to have a definite
meaning.

the way - Once again, we can
only guess at what Crane
means. Presumably, he is
talking about the answers to life.

I am lost - Again, presumably, he
is talking about a mentor who
cannot even guide himself.

heart; warm

Possible answer: It makes us
feel good to have money.

No, not really. The meaning is
just too obscure.

Poet's Corner

Robert Frost was born on March 26, 1874 in San Francisco, California. After his father's death, the family moved to Massachusetts. He spent most of his life in New England; thereby Vermont claiming him as its state poet laureate. Although his poetic career was not fully recognized until he was about forty, he attained many honors and awards during his lifetime. Perhaps Frost's most notable appearance was at the inauguration of John F. Kennedy as he recited "The Gift Outright."

Robert Frost's poetry is full of simple wisdom. However, if one looks deeper into his poetry, a wealth of the elusive meanings in life can be found. At first glance, Frost's poetry may appear optimistic, but his personal life was not an easy one.

Frost died on January 29, 1963, in Boston.

1. a. Read the poem "Mending Wall" found on page 235.

   b. It must be recognized that rhyme is not essential to poetry. Although the sounds of words are important to the poet, real poetry exists in the meanings of words, not in their sounds. The emphasis on meaning is more important today than ever before.

      Look at the form of the poem. Consider the number of stanzas and lines, metrical pattern, and rhyme scheme. Is there any regular pattern?

   c. Poetry is usually written in rhymed, blank, or free verse. We have looked at rhymed verses in previous lessons.

      Blank verse is a form of poetry that uses unrhymed iambic pentameter. (See Lesson 26, **1c**) It was commonly used by Shakespeare, John Milton in his works *Paradise Lost* and *Paradise Regained* and was later popularized by William Wordsworth and Samuel Coleridge. Blank verse is a predecessor of free verse.

      Free verse does not contain any patterns of meter, rhyme, or stanza. However, free verse may use repetitive patterns of words, phrases, or other elements. We will discuss free verse further in Lesson 31.

d. Contemporary poets avoid rhyme for several reasons:

1) If the poet follows a rhyme scheme, he must restrict
    himself only to those words which fit the rhyme scheme.
    This might force him to use a word which fits the rhyme
    scheme, but does not quite express his real meaning, and
    therefore distorts the message.
2) Repetitious rhyme creates a song-like effect. Most poets
    feel that this lowers the dignity of their work to the level
    of nursery rhymes or top forty tunes.
3) Rhyme is distracting to the reader and can cause the
    reader to become absorbed in the rhyme scheme and
    ignore the content of the poetry.

Most contemporary poets do not use rhyme. However, if
they use rhyme at all, they take great care to make the
rhyme unobtrusive — almost unnoticeable — and they
make it subordinate to the meaning of the poem.

e. Try writing a poem using blank verse.

2. a. Read again, the poem, "Mending Wall," found on page 235.

b. Lines 1-11 and lines 12-22 are like two paragraphs.
    Summarize, in your own words, what ideas Frost is
    introducing in these first two segments.

c. Why does Frost call it an outdoor game?

d. From lines 2-3 and 30-35, there are four main objections that
    Frost raises against the wall. Summarize these objections in
    your own words.

e. Why does Frost say that his neighbor moves in darkness in
    line 41?

f. What does line 43 suggest?

g. A **symbol** is something which stands for something else. The symbol itself must be an object, but it can represent an abstraction. Often times, a symbol brings with it many associations. For example, the cross is the most recognizable and complex symbol in Western Civilization. It can stand for abstractions, such as holiness, or it can stand for something concrete, such as Jesus as the Savior.

The wall in "Mending Wall" is a symbol. What do you think it stands for?

h. Robert Frost read this poem in 1962 to an audience in Russia. Consider the political climate of that time. What further symbolism do you see?

i. Try writing a poem today using symbolism. You will have time tomorrow to complete it.

3. a. Read "Stopping by Woods on a Snowy Evening" found on page 249.

b. What is the rhyme scheme?

c. Describe the circumstances which Frost creates in the first three stanzas.

d. In the last stanza, Frost says he must be moving on. What is he moving on toward?

Is sleep a symbol?

e. If necessary, complete the poem you started yesterday.

4. a. Read the poem "Birches," found on page 237. There are no tough symbols or difficult poetic devices to plow through. You should be able to derive a good interpretation of this poem on your own. Have fun with it.

b. "Birches" is full of rich imagery. Remember, an image is not just visual. An image can contain responses to any of the five senses.

Read the first thirteen lines of the poem again. List all the words that create a sensual response other than visual. Beside each word, write your response. For example, perhaps the first words which create a sensual response are ice storms in line five. Ice storms suggest cold. Continue listing the words.
Ex: ice storms - cold

c. Try writing a poem full of imagery. You will have time tomorrow if necessary.

a. Read "The Road Not Taken" found on page 250. This is one of Frost's most famous poems.

b. What situation does Frost describe in the first two stanzas?

c. What is the dilemma that he faces in stanza three?

d. Have you ever felt this way? Discuss this with your teacher.

e. What does he mean by the last two lines of the poem?

f. Do you think it is fair of Frost to leave the poem unended and to never tell us what difference his choice has made? Be honest with this question.

g. Does Frost himself know if his choice really did make all the difference?

h. We make many choices in life. What are some choices you have had to make?

You will be making more choices about your life's direction after you finish high school. Many high school athletes quit pursuing their sports once they leave high school. Although they could continue to develop their skills, they choose to go to college, find a civilian job, enlist in the military, etc. Ask your parents (or other significant elder) what choices they have had to make. Ask them what they would have done differently if circumstances would have allowed. How can you apply their experience to your own life?

i. If you need to, complete the poem you started yesterday.

1.

b. This poem is not in any recognizable form such as a sonnet, repeating stanza, or rhyme scheme. The only repeating pattern is iambic pentameter.

2.

b. Lines 1-11 - The wall is unnatural. The forces of nature, the hunters, and the dogs are all trying to bring the wall down. Lines 12-22 - The wall separates the two men. Ironically, repairing the wall seems to be their only common bond.

c. He thinks the wall is ridiculous, but his neighbor takes it seriously.

d.
1) Lines two and three suggest that nature itself doesn't like the wall.
2) There are no animals to keep controlled.
3) The wall might offend people.
4) Walls get a negative response from things.

e. Frost doesn't know the man — he's a mystery because he won't let Frost get to know him personally.

f. The neighbor's desire to keep the wall is a tradition that he keeps without even thinking about it.

g. Hopefully, answers will be varied and complex for this question. Anything which mentions the walls people put up to keep out other people, emotions, beliefs, etc., is an appropriate answer.

h. Possibly, the walls which world powers put up in response to their fears.

3.

b. aaba, bbcb, ccdc, dddd
Notice this is not a regular form. Frost made it up.

c. The poet is riding horseback through the woods on a winter evening. It is snowing, but evidently not storming. He is apparently enjoying the ride because he stops to take in the scenery. He paints a peaceful picture in which anyone would likely be stimulated to think about his life and circumstances, as people tend to do when they are alone in a quiet, restful setting.

d. sleep

Yes, it is symbolic of death.

4.

b.
Line 6 - ice and winter - cold
Line 7 - after a rain - wetness; fresh fragrance after a rain
Line 7 - click - this is an auditory image
Line 8 - the breeze rises - this can be felt and heard
Line 9 - cracks - this is an auditory image
Line 10 - sun's warmth - this is tactile (related to the sense of touch)
Line 11 - (the entire line can be heard as well as seen)

5.

b. He has come to a fork in the road while walking in the woods.

. He doesn't think he will pass that way again and doesn't know which road is better. He wants to take both.

. To say that it has made all the difference doesn't really tell us anything. We will never know why. Therefore, we only presume that Frost is suggesting that it is a good thing not to conform to the conventional ways of doing things. We can only guess at this, however.

Answers will vary. Allow for discussion.

. No. He doesn't know where the other path would have taken him.

. Allow for discussion.

The Descriptive Essay

Refer to Lessons 21-22 to help you in writing a general essa[y]

1. a. Some of the poems you have read should have stimulated your thinking. Your assignment this week is to write a **descriptive essay** on one of the poems. Look over the poems and make your selection. Read and analyze the poem until you feel you have a good understanding. Now think of a topic for your descriptive essay. This can be an object, an impression or idea, or a person. For example, you might choose "The Road Not Taken" by Robert Frost and discuss the effects of the choices we make in life.

   b. Write a thesis statement. Make your thesis statement specif[ic]. This will help you keep on track. Remember, as in the expository essay, every sentence should support the thesis statement.

2. a. Think about what you are going to say about your topic. Write down ideas as they come.

   b. What sensory details add clarity to your topic?

   c. List the parts of the poem that support your topic.

3. This kind of brainstorming is helpful because when ideas come, they often go just as quickly unless they are written down. Furthermore, as you look at your ideas on the page[,] it will stimulate the imagination to generate more ideas. Keep working until you have a page full of ideas, more tha[n] you will need. Then leave it to use tomorrow.

4. Look at the ideas you wrote yesterday and organize them. You should be able to identify topics, subtopics, and even details and examples that fit within the subtopics. Create a[n] informal outline based on the ideas you listed yesterday.

Now you are ready to write a rough draft. As in the expository essay, you may find it helpful to write the body paragraphs first.

Using your thesis statement as a focal point, expand on the ideas presented. List examples that illustrate your thesis.

Write the introductory paragraph and concluding paragraph. Continue to work on your rough draft. Writing takes time. Give yourself several days to write a rough draft of your essay.

Edit your paper for grammar, punctuation, and spelling. Write your final draft.

Essay Assessment II

To help you assess your student's essay, complete the following checklist.

The essay contains:

1) a thesis statement that clearly identifies the main idea   _____

2) an introductory paragraph   _____

3) body paragraphs that support the main idea   _____

4) a concluding paragraph   _____

5) a topic sentence for each paragraph   _____

6) sentences within a paragraph that relate back to the topic sentence _____

7) transitional words to relate one sentence to the next   _____

8) a reworded thesis statement in the concluding paragraph   _____

9) cohesiveness and unity   _____

10) correct grammar, punctuation, and spelling   _____

If your student has missed any of the above points, encourage him to go back and improve his essay. Congratulate him for his effort and completion.

oet's Corner

William Carlos Williams (1883-1963) practiced as a pediatrician in New Jersey before he began writing. He wrote stories and plays as well as poetry. He was inspired by the postimpressionist works in the visual arts. In 1963, he was awarded a posthumous Pulitzer Prize for *Pictures from Brueghel and Other Poems*, a collection of verse. (You will learn more about Brueghel in this lesson.) He is probably most noted for *Paterson*, a collection of poetry.

. a. Read the poem, "Queen-Ann's-Lace," found on page 326.

b. Words to know:
   1) anemone - a plant with showy, colorful flowers
   2) pious - having religious, often pretentious, devotion

c. What is Queen-Ann's-Lace?

d. Look for a rhyme scheme. Count the number of lines and count the number of syllables per line. Is there a recognizable form to this poem?

e. Poetry without a recognizable form is called **free verse**. In Lesson 28, you learned that free verse has no rhyme scheme, no prescribed line length, no regular stanzas, etc. The poet is free to choose the words he wants and arrange them any way that he wants. He is free to convey his meaning in precise language and not restricted to formulas involving rhyme, meter, etc. Therefore, the poet must use true poetic devices such as imagery, metaphor, repetitive patterns of words and phrases, and word selection rather than artificial conventions.

f. In line 12, Williams switches from *her* to *his*. To whom do you think the *he* and *she* of the poem refer?

g. Do you think Williams believed in God?

h. With the coming of free verse, which was popularized by the publication of T.S. Eliot's "The Waste Land" in 1921, also came freedom in choosing subject matter for a poem. Today's poets do not consider great subjects, such as love, philosophy, or religion to be essential to poetry. A poem can consist of images which describe an object — and need not be any deeper than that, although most poets try to convey more than just an image. Furthermore, today's poets regard any subject as suitable for a poem and are not concerned with public taste. Thus, we see poems about the dark side of human nature alongside more upbeat subjects. We must not scoff at this. When people begin writing poetry, they tend to write about the painful experiences first. This is a good place to start since strong feelings often generate strong poems.

i. Try writing your own poem today using free verse.

2. a. Read "The Dance" found on page 322.

b. What form does this poem have — rhymed, blank, or free verse?

c. Is there a symbol or other deeper significance to the poem?

d. The poem refers to one of Brueghel's paintings. Using a reference book, computer, or the library, find a little information about Pieter Brueghel, the Elder. Pieter Brueghel, the Elder, (1525-1569) was a Flemish artist well known for his paintings of countryfolk in realistic scenes. He rejected the influences of Italian Renaissance and portrayed realistic figures in natural peasant life. (Later in life, Brueghel changed his name to Bruegel.)

4. "The Kermess," which Williams refers to in this poem is a type of festival. Using a reference book, computer, or the library, find a print of *The Peasant Dance*, Brueghel's painting in which "The Kermess" is shown. Study the painting. Look at the entire scene and then look at each character. Study their facial expressions and bodies. Focus on the details of the people and their surroundings. Take time and appreciate the painting. Now, write your own poem describing the painting. Remember, your images can include taste, smell, sound, and touch, as well as the visual.

(An excellent resource on the history of art, which includes this print, is *Art Through the Ages*, published by Harcourt Brace Janovich ISBN 0-15-503763-3.)

a. Read "By the Road to the Contagious Hospital" found on page 325.

b. Once again, Williams is trying to describe something. What is he describing?

c. Stanza four describes a turning point in the poem. What change does the poem make in stanza four?

d. Select five or six words or phrases from the first three stanzas which capture the images of winter.

e. Select five or six words or phrases from the last three stanzas which suggest spring.

f. How does Williams compare and contrast the images of winter and spring?

g. Why has Williams done this?

h. Write your own poem about spring.

1.

c. Queen-Ann's-Lace is a wild plant with delicate white flowers in flat-topped clusters.

d. No.

f. *He* is a reference to God, the maker of the flower; *she* is a reference to the flower.

g. Williams refers to *he* as the maker of the flower. However, *he* is not capitalized, and the ending of the poem suggests that such thoughts about a maker might be nothing at all. This is a tough question, but my guess is that Williams had a sort of resigned belief in God as if belief in a higher being made sense to him, but he didn't really know for sure.

2.

b. It is free verse. Although Williams tends to use nine syllables per line, this is just his own device.

c. No.

5.

b. He describes the coming of spring. There is no further mystery to the poem.

c. We get the first indication of the vegetation growing rather than lying dormant in winter.

d.
1) a cold wind
2) (wind) from the northeast
3) brown (fields and weeds)
4) twiggy bushes
5) small trees (twiggy suggests there are no leaves)
6) brown leaves
7) leafless vines

e.
1) They enter
2) now the grass
3) curl of wildcarrot leaf
4) It quickens
5) outline of leaf
6) they grip down
7) begin to awaken

f. Williams wants to contrast the lifelessness of winter with the emerging life of spring. To do this, he sets up a contrast involving dull color to lively color, lack of movement to motion, and formlessness to shape.

g. This is what really happens when spring comes. This is a fine poem, but it isn't anything more than a description.

Poet's Corner

John Crowe Ransom was born in 1888 in Pulaski, Tennessee. He admired the poetry of John Donne and other metaphysical poets of the 17th century. His poetry is marked with irony and often deals with the inevitability of human decay. For the most part, his poetry adheres to meter, rhyme, and stanza. Along with his poetry, he is remembered as a teacher and critic. Ransom died in 1974.

a. Read "Bells for John Whiteside's Daughter" found on page 389.

b. Words to know:
   1) bruited - reported
   2) harried - destroyed or plundered

c. Look at the form of the poem. What is the rhyme scheme?

d. How many lines are in the stanzas?

e. Ransom uses the phrase "brown study" two times. How does Ransom use this phrase to show us the little girl's characteristics? A good dictionary should have the definition of brown study.

f. How do we know that the little girl is dead?

g. Ransom gives us very little physical description of the girl. Is he cheating us?

h. Try to write a description of the girl. (How old is she? Is she a rich girl? Is she smart? What did she look like?) These are only a few questions you might answer. Create a complete characterization of her based on the poem.

i. Ransom doesn't dwell on the girl's passing. He only shows us glimpses of before and after. Do you find this effective? Would it be better for him to give a detailed description of how she died and what the funeral was like? Defend you answer.

. a. Read "Blue Girls" found on page 396.

   b. Words to know:
     1) sward - a grassy ground
     2) blear - to dim or to blur (as with tears)

   c. Look at the form of this poem. What is the rhyme scheme?

   d. How many lines are in the stanzas?

   e. Who are the blue girls?

   f. To whom is this poem really addressed?

   g. Have you ever thought about how you would look at things if you were in your parents' place? Put yourself in their place for a day or two. You might observe them and ask questions regarding what they think about and how they see the future for themselves and for you. Use your information to write two paragraphs. For example, in the first paragraph, you may write about why your parents take things seriously and are so conservative. In the second paragraph, write about why you do not take things as seriously as they do.

3. a. Read "Janet Waking" found on page 403.

   b. Words to know:
     1) transmogrifying - changing into a different (fantastic) form
     2) droning - making a continuous humming noise
     3) implored - asked earnestly

   c. What is the difference between this poem and "Bells for Whiteside's Daughter"?

   d. What is a Christian's response to death? Use Scripture to support your answer.

4. Use today to read various poetry selections of your choice.

5. Reading poetry inspires the poetic nature in all of us. Spend time today writing a poem using any topic and style you desire.

.

c. The rhyme scheme is abab.

d. It consists of five four-line stanzas. The form was created by Ransom.

e. "Brown study" means deep in thought or reverie. Reverie contrasts the activity of the little girl. Everything now appears lifeless and still. The geese, likewise, are lazy without her to disturb them.

We know she is dead because the bells are a farewell, and she will not return.

f. This is subject to opinion, but Ransom describes her well by telling us what she did and how she acted.

a. You're on your own on this one but the following may be helpful. - Her little body and the lightness of her footfall indicate she was young, small, and delicate. - Her speed and her tireless heart give us an image of an energetic, lively young girl. - Her wars, taking up arms, and harrying show us a strong-willed child. - The fact that she had a pond, orchard, and geese tells us she was probably wealthy.

Again, this is subject to opinion, but Ransom's use of the power of suggestion is stronger than the gory details.

2.

c. The first three stanzas are abba; the fourth stanza is ababa.

d. The first three stanzas are four lines and the fourth stanza is five lines. The form was created by Ransom.

e. Apparently, the blue girls are young, pretty girls who are accustomed to high society.

f. The poem is addressed to all of us because everyone who experiences the physical blessings of youth also experiences his own decline, should one live long enough.

g. Allow for creative expression.

3.

c. In "Whiteside's Daughter," the girl is dead. In this poem, Janet learns about death. Also, in "Whiteside's Daughter," Ransom reflects on the girl. In this poem, Janet reflects on her rooster's death.

d. Helpful Scriptures - I Thes. 4:14; Rev. 14:13; Phil. 1:21; Isa. 57:1-2; II Tim. 4:8

Poet's Corner

Edward Estlin Cummings, better known as **e e cummings**, was born in Cambridge, Massachusetts in 1894. (The odd manner in which he wrote his name is due to his experimentation in syntax. This will be explained in **1b**.) He wrote journals, prose, and plays as well as poetry. His first published book, *The Enormous Room*, came out of his disturbing experiences during World War I. After the war, he studied painting in Paris and continued writing. Much of his writing came out of his hatred for bureaucracy and his own deeply painful life. Cummings, one of America's creative contemporary poets, died in 1962.

1. a. Read "Spring is like a perhaps hand" found on page 446.

    b. Cummings exploited the liberty of free verse and experimented with the mechanics of punctuation, form, and syntax.

       Syntax is the way words are put together to form phrases and sentences. His experiments with punctuation and form are considered excessive by today's standards. Contemporary poets are usually careful to observe conventions for sentence structure and mechanics; however, we can appreciate Cummings' clever experiments. The main value of these gimmicks, as one might call them, is to get the reader to concentrate harder on the content of the poem, and to enlarge the content of the poem by seeing words from a different angle. The effectiveness of this is questionable. However, we have one reaction to *red blood*, and another reaction to *blood-red*. Therefore, our natural speech habits recognize that there is some value in rearranging words to obtain a slightly different meaning. Furthermore, we tend to respond to CHOLESTEROL with alarm; and not so to *cholesterol*. Therefore, today's poets use their freedoms occasionally, but they do so in good taste, to enhance the content of the poem rather than risk taking away from the content.

    c. Rearrange the poem in your mind or on paper to get a clearer understanding of the poem. For example, you might read the first line as: Spring is like a hand, perhaps.

d. What is the main difference between this poem and Williams' "By the Road to the Contagious Hospital"?

e. Cummings shows us someone concerned about the window at spring. How is this effective in suggesting excitement about the spring season?

f. Compare the imagery of this poem with Williams' "By the Road to the Contagious Hospital." Which images are stronger for you?

a. Read "i thank You God for most this amazing" found on page 448.

b. If necessary, put in punctuation and rearrange words to help in understanding the poem.

c. What does Cummings mean by the sun's birthday in line six?

d. What does line five suggest?

e. How do the expressions *ears of my ears* and *eyes of my eyes* emphasize Cummings' awareness level?

f. Write a poem of thanksgiving. You may want to experiment with syntax.

In yesterday's poem, "i thank You God for most this amazing," Cummings is so overcome by nature and his natural senses that he attributes this to God. Find some passages from Scripture that refer to this. Read and meditate on this today. Write your own poem expressing awe of God and His creation. Look in the Psalms for suggestions. You will have time tomorrow to complete your poem.

a. Read "anyone lived in a pretty how town" found on page 460.

b. If necessary, put in punctuation and rearrange words to help in understanding the poem.

c. This poem can be unraveled up to a point, but rearranging words and providing punctuation is not completely satisfactory. For example, we have to accept line four at face value. Try to imagine what Cummings is saying.

d. Cummings declares that this is a pretty town. Are there any details in the poem that describe the town?

e. Cummings interjects references to the seasons, elements, etc. What does this suggest?

f. What is this poem about?

g. If you need to, complete the poem you began yesterday.

5. Today, read over the poems you read this week, or find other poetry of Cummings. Try writing your own poem. Experiment with punctuation, syntax, and form. Have fun.

1.

c. Allow for creative expression.

d. "By the Road to the Contagious Hospital" - Williams shows us spring coming by showing the changes in the weather, plants, etc.
"Spring is like a perhaps hand" - Cummings shows us a glimpse of what people do when spring comes.

e. Concern about the details of the window sill suggests preparation, excitement, and a sense of continually looking out to see if something is happening.

f. This is subject to opinion, but Williams' "By the Road to the Contagious Hospital" gives us an actual glimpse and feeling for spring.

2.

c. Each day is a new beginning.

d. Each day is like beginning life afresh.

e. It adds emphasis, like saying that our goosebumps have goosebumps.

4.

d. Not really. Cummings is describing life in the town, not the town itself.

e. This suggests the passing of time without noticing it.

f. The people in this town live their lives superficially, never noticing the real things of life. They are all the same, therefore, and no one seems to care about anything real. They seem to want to be like one another.

The Narrative Essay

   a. Cummings' "anyone lived in a pretty how town" referred to people living their lives superficially. Everyone seemed to be doing the same thing and lacked individuality. Does this poem relate to any groups of people you have been acquainted with, such as children at school, church groups, Scouts, Little League, etc.? Have you ever felt compelled to do things you don't want to do in order to be accepted by a group or even just one other person?

   b. This is a good question for a narrative essay. The **narrative essay** tells a story, usually from the writer's own experience. It is presented in a connected sequence of events. The event may be factual or fiction. The main purpose of the narrative essay is to tell what happened.

   c. Identify your topic and follow the general essay guidelines in Lessons 21-22 to write your narrative essay.

Essay Assessment III

To help you assess your student's essay, complete the following checklist.

The essay contains:

1) a thesis statement that clearly identifies the main idea   _____

2) an introductory paragraph   _____

3) body paragraphs that support the main idea   _____

4) a concluding paragraph   _____

5) a topic sentence for each paragraph   _____

6) sentences within a paragraph that relate back to the topic sentence _____

7) transitional words to relate one sentence to the next   _____

8) a reworded thesis statement in the concluding paragraph   _____

9) cohesiveness and unity   _____

10) correct grammar, punctuation, and spelling   _____

If your student has missed any of the above points, encourage him to go back and improve his essay. Congratulate him for his effort and completion.

Poet's Corner

Wystan Hugh Auden was born in England in 1907. He lived in Germany for some time before moving to the United States. Auden's association with a group of leftist writers brought him much attention. He became an American citizen in 1946. At about this time, Auden had a spiritual reawakening and returned to Anglicanism. Two years later, he received the Pulitzer prize for his collection of poems, *The Age of Anxiety*. This collection revealed the return of his boyhood religion. Auden's influence was apparent in the uprising new poets. He died in 1973. Auden remains one of the most important American writers.

1. a. Read "Musée des Beaux Arts" found on page 507.

   b. Like an opening paragraph, the first five lines of the poem tell us the subject of the poem. What is the subject of this poem?

   c. Do we have to know who The Old Masters are in line two in order to understand the meaning of the poem?

   d. Who are The Old Masters?

   e. How should a Christian respond to human suffering? Find Scripture to support your answer.

   f. Write a poem that expresses the scriptural Christian response.

2. a. Many writers make reference to artists and their works. It is expected that the reader be familiar with these works of art. In Lesson 31, you found out some information about Pieter Brueghel, the Elder. Using a reference book, computer, or library, find out who Icarus was.

b. Read other poems by W.H. Auden.

. a. Using a reference book, computer, or library, find Brueghel's painting, *The Landscape with the Fall of Icarus.* Take your time and study the painting. Look at each character. Look at the fine detail in his work. Does this painting help you understand the poem or does the poem help you understand the painting?

b. Read more poetry of your choice.

. Look at other paintings by Brueghel or other artists of your choice. Select a painting that interests you. Study the painting and then write a poem.

. a. Read "The Unknown Citizen" found on page 507.

b. Reread Cummings' "anyone lived in a pretty how town" found on page 460.

c. Compare the two poems.

d. Although the two poems treat the same subject, they go about it differently. Cite two major ways in which the poems treat the same subject differently.

e. Which poem do you think is more effective? Do you think that Cummings or Auden was more directly talking to you personally? Why?

f. Write a poem using any style you wish.

1.

b. There is great human suffering all around us, yet we go on with life and don't notice.

c. No.

d. Master painters

e. Possible references: Matt. 5:7; Rom. 12:8; Heb. 4:16; Col. 3:12

2.

a. In Greek mythology, Icarus and his father, Daedalus, were imprisoned in a labyrinth by King Minos. Daedalus made wax wings for himself and Icarus. They tried to escape, but Icarus flew too closely to the sun which caused his wings to melt. He fell into the sea and drowned.

5.

c. Both poems are about people who have no real identity. The people seem to live life without experiencing it.

d. Cummings looks at a town; Auden looks at the one person. Cummings speaks in generalities; Auden goes into details.

e. Answers will differ, but my guess is adults will choose Auden, whereas students are likely to choose Cummings.

Literary Terms

abstractions - generalities which have no specific meaning

allegory - a description that has a double meaning, one literal and the other figurative

allusion – a brief reference to a story, person, or idea that an author uses to recall emotion or context

blank verse - a form of poetry that uses unrhymed iambic pentameter

character – a person who appears in a story

climax – the turning point, or action peak of the plot

compare – illustrate how two ideas, characters, or stories are alike

concrete – in poetry, the opposite of abstract; words that create images

conflict – the element of a story that involves an obstacle that must be overcome

context clues – the words that appear in a sentence surrounding a difficult word that helps to understand the meaning of that word

contrast – illustrate how two ideas, characters, or stories are different

descriptive essay – an essay that emphasizes the characteristics of a person, place, or idea

dialect – language and expressions that are peculiar to a certain group of people

direct characterization – a characterization method that describes the character by what he does and says

editorializing – a technique an author uses to add his own interpretation of events of a story

exposition – the element of a story that introduces the characters and explains the background of the story, setting, and the present situation

expository essay – an essay that sets forth information and explains a given topic

external conflict – the conflict of the character's struggle with outside forces

falling action – the element of a story when the action of the turning point is worked out and a solution is at hand

first person point of view – a story written in this view is limited to one character's view using the pronoun *I*

flat character – an unchanging, one-dimensional character

foreshadowing – the method used by an author to give hints to the reader of upcoming events

free verse – form of poetry that does not contain any patterns of meter, rhyme, or stanza

iambic foot – poetry which contains the pattern of one unstressed and one stressed syllable

iambic pentameter – poetry which consists of five iambic feet per line

idiom – a phrase or expression that is recognized to have a different meaning from what it literally says

imagery – a literary device used by an author to create a picture in the mind of the reader through the use of descriptive words and phrases

implied metaphor – a figure of speech that compares two things which are not usually related; the comparison is never stated, but implied

indirect characterization – a characterization method that describes the character by giving mere details involving height, weight, hair color, etc.

internal conflict – the conflict of the character's struggle within himself

irony – a literary device that reveals a reality other than what seems to be true

metaphor – a figure of speech that compares two things which are not usually related

metrical pattern – a poem's pattern determined by the type of feet and number of lines

mood – the feeling the author desires to create in the reader

narrative essay – an essay that tells a story, presented in a connected sequence of events

narrator – the person who tells the story

octave – the first eight lines of a sonnet

personification – a figure of speech which gives human attributes to something that is not human

plot – the sequence of events and actions that take place in a story. Every good plot contains: exposition, rising action, climax, falling action, and resolution.

plot line – a graphic representation of the elements of a plot

point of view – the position the author takes in order to tell the story

quatrain – in a sonnet, two quatrains make up an octave; a four-line stanza

realism – literature that describes a story within a realistic view of life

resolution – the part of the story in which the solution comes to a conclusion, and the problem is solved

rhyme scheme – the pattern of rhyme at the end of lines

rising action – the element of a story that consists of a series of problems and struggles which build toward a climax

romanticism – literature that describes a story based more on an imaginary view of life

round character – a well-developed, many sided character

second person point of view – used when the author addresses the reader throughout a story, and the pronoun *you* is used

sestet – the last six lines of a sonnet

setting – the time and place where the story takes place

short story – a fictional writing in prose form that has a limited number of characters, brings forth a single emotional effect, and can usually be read in a single sitting

simile – a figure of speech which makes a comparison between two things by using words such as *like* and *as*

sonnet – poetry usually consisting of fourteen lines, and usually written in iambic pentameter

stanza – in poetry, grouping of lines set off by a space usually following a pattern of meter and rhyme

stream-of-consciousness – the technique of developing a character's thoughts as they occur

suspense – a technique an author uses to help keep the reader interested in the story

symbol – that which stands for something else

syntax – the way words are put together to form phrases and sentences

tercet – in a sonnet, two tercets make up a sestet; a three-line stanza

theme – the idea or statement which a story is about

thesis statement – the sentence in an essay that states the main idea or purpose

third person limited omniscient – a third person point of view that falls anywhere between the omniscient and objective points of view

third person objective – a third person point of view that allows the author to merely report the characters and events

third person omniscient – a third person point of view that allows the author to have a God-like position over the story by telling what the characters feel and why they act a certain way

third person point of view – a story written in this view is told from an all-knowing outside source, and the pronouns *he* and *she* are used

transitional words or phrases – words or phrases that help relate one sentence to the next

Bibliography

Crane, Stephen. *The Red Badge of Courage*. New York: Random House, 1983.

Hemingway, Ernest. *The Old Man and the Sea*. New York: Simon & Schuster, 1980.

Stegner, Wallace and Mary, eds. *Great American Short Stories*. New York: Random House, 1985.

Steinbeck, John. *The Pearl*. New York: Penguin Group, 1945.

Williams, Oscar and Honig, Edwin, eds. *The Mentor Book of Major American Poets*. New York: Penguin Group, 1962.

Congratulations,

You Are Part Of The *Common Sense Press* Family.

Now you can receive our FREE e-mail newsletter, containing:
- Teaching Tips
- Product Announcements
- Helpful Hints from Veteran Homeschoolers
- & Much More!

Please take a moment to register with us.

Common Sense Press
Product Registration
8786 Highway 21
Melrose, FL 32666

Or online at
www.commonsensepress.com/register

After registering, search our site for teaching tips, product information, and ways to get more from your *Common Sense Press* purchase.

Your Name _____

Your E-Mail Address _____

Your Address _____

City _____ State _____ Zip _____

Product Purchased _____

From What Company Did You Purchase This Product? _____

Get involved with the *Common Sense Press* community.
Visit our web site often to contribute your ideas, read what others are doing teaching their children, see new teaching tips, and more.